HOW TO BE A GROWNUP

Heather,

Best of luck in all
you do— You will definitely
"leave your mark" and have
fun doing it.

Love,
Grandpa Al &
Gramma Kathy

HOW TO BE A GROWNUP

247 Lab-tested Strategies
for Conquering the World

Margaret Feinberg and Leif Oines

W PUBLISHING GROUP
A Division of Thomas Nelson Publishers
Since 1798

www.wpublishinggroup.com

Published by W Publishing Group, a Division of Thomas Nelson, Inc., P.O. Box 141000, Nashville, Tennessee 37214.

Library of Congress Cataloging-in-Publication Data

Feinberg, Margaret, 1974-
    How to be a grownup: 247 lab-tested strategies for conquering the world/by Margaret Feinberg and Leif Oines.
        p. cm.
    Includes bibliographical references and index.
    ISBN 0-8499-0417-X
    1. Young adults—Life skills guides. 2. Life skills. 3. Interpersonal relations. I. Oines, Leif. II. Title.
    HQ799.5.F45 2005
    646.7'084'2--dc22

2004029450

Printed in the United States of America

05 06 07 RRD 9 8 7 6 5 4 3 2 1

To all the people, too numerous to name here,
who have invested in our lives and put up with us when we made
a bunch of stupid mistakes or didn't listen to your good advice.

Thank you.

WORK

LIVING ARRANGEMENTS

FRIENDSHIPS

THE BLING-BLING

HEALTH

LIFE SURVIVAL SKILLS 101

INTRODUCTION

You might be wondering about the claims of lab testing in the title.

[Note: For the record, no animals were harmed in the making of this book.]

While we didn't put on long white coats, spend countless hours looking under a microscope, or even step foot inside a scientific research center, we have been spending the last few years trying to figure out exactly what people meant when they told us to "grow up."

So our lab has been our lives—whether in Florida, North Carolina, Texas, Colorado, Alaska, Honduras, Spain, or all the other places we've lived and visited in between. We have been the subjects of this experiment. Now no one is perfect, and we don't claim to have all the answers about growing up or even being a grownup, but we've had a lot of fun experimenting so far. Our hope is that you'll learn to enjoy life a little more after laughing at our mistakes and hearing our gripes about having to become an adult.

May God bless you and the people around you with the grace that it takes to survive and thrive as a grownup.

RELATIONSHIPS

Part I: Still Single?

Do you ever get tired of annoying questions about your single status? If so, you're not alone. You'd think people in relationships would be a little more sensitive to those without one, but often they just don't think before they ask. So the next time someone asks you why you're still single, here are five responses that might come in handy:

QUESTION: WHY ARE YOU STILL SINGLE?

ANSWERS:

➤ I can't give away that secret. You'll just have to tune in to next Friday night's *Unsolved Mysteries* and watch the exposé like everyone else.

➤ I think it might have something to do with my parents' obsession with teaching me not to talk to strangers.

➤ Well, this is just a guess, but rumor has it that my standards are too high. I just refuse to settle. Know what I mean? Wait . . . oops, of course you don't. [You can say this because a hastily conducted unscientific poll shows that 98 percent of people who ask this question are already married.]

➤ Honestly, I ask myself that every single night as I lie down with hot tears streaming down my lonely face in a cold bed all by myself, contemplating the despair of having no one to share pillow talk or anything else I've seen on TV with and realizing there's just no hope for ever finding that life companion, soul mate, and best friend. I know the person must exist out there somewhere. [This is best delivered with dramatic facial expressions of intense pain and the whiniest voice you can generate.]

➤ I just haven't found anyone who deserves me yet. [Beware: This answer can be interpreted as both incredibly egotistical and unbelievably self-deprecating.]

Part II: How's Married Life?

If you happen to be one of those rare people who decided to get married right out of the womb, or at least while still under the average marrying age, then you'll probably get hit with the possible all-time favorite or least favorite question [depending on how things are going with your spouse that day]:

QUESTION: SO, HOW IS MARRIED LIFE?

ANSWERS:

➤ You tell me. You've been married longer than I have. [This is particularly effective if the inquiring person is married.]

➤ I could tell you, but then I'd have to kill you. [This is most effective if the inquiring person is single.]

➤ Didn't you hear? We got divorced right after the honeymoon. But thanks for bringing it up! [Granted, this is not true, but it will be really fun to watch the uncomfortable look of regret sweep over the person's face. You could be saving countless other newlyweds from having to endure this question in the future—'cause that person will think twice before asking it again!]

➤ Well, I'll tell ya, buddy . . . there is no premarital counseling, how-to book, parent-child talk, or Crest commercial in the world that prepared me for morning breath.

➤ So far, so good. I'm giving it another few months before I take the checkbook and credit card and head off to Tahiti.

➤ Married life is great, and the sex is even better! [Yes, this is a little off-color. But really . . . what do they want you to say when they ask this question? Why not give 'em the good stuff you know their prying little mind is longing for!]

Single Serving, Anyone?

Picture yourself married. Think of all the time, energy, and commitment it requires. Until that day comes, why not make the most of the time you've been given right now and invest in other people and your own spiritual growth?

NOW IS THE TIME TO TAKE ADVANTAGE OF THE FREEDOM YOU HAVE IN HOW YOU USE YOUR TIME AND ENERGY.

Consider these fulfilling, difference-making, fly-by-the-seat-of-your-pants, fun ways to serve while you're able to do whatever you want:

Volunteer in your church nursery or a local day care.
Let's face it. When you get married and have children of your own, the last thing you're going to want to do in your spare time is take care of other people's children on top of your full-time child-rearing responsibilities. This will give you great practice and will also be a huge blessing to the parents of those little bundles of joy with limitless energy.

Participate in overseas evangelism opportunities.
Countless missions agencies have short-term programs for singles. Consider serving overseas while you can still go without uprooting a whole family. Many closed-access countries will not permit overt missionary activity but will allow single Christian students or professionals to come in and teach English without any special degrees or requirements. Spend time making friends with the nationals, and you'll make a difference in their lives. It will amaze you when they begin to ask why you have peace in your heart, or a smile on your face, or a desire to help others instead of yourself.

Host dinner parties.
There are so many people who need to get a life. Don't just sit around and think about how pathetic they are [or you are!]. Invite them over and help them hop on the clue train toward good social graces. Use small gatherings to help timid people feel more comfortable. On another night, invite all the loud, obnoxious people you know and watch them fight it out for all the attention on center stage. You'll be entertained *and* be fostering community at the same time!

He Said, She Heard

Ever feel like you're not getting through? Like you're saying one thing, and the gal is hearing something completely different? Here's a short guide for those kinds of moments:

HE SAID	SHE HEARD
"Wanna grab dinner?"	"What should we name our first child?"
"Nothing's wrong . . . why?"	"I don't feel comfortable enough to share my intimate thoughts with you."
"I'm going out with the guys."	"You aren't fun enough or cool enough to meet my needs."
"You look great in that dress!"	"Every other dress you've ever worn makes you look fat."
"Let's just be friends."	"I hate you!"

She Said, **He Heard**

Not communicating well goes both ways. You say one thing, and the guy hears something completely different. Here's a short guide for those kinds of moments:

SHE SAID	HE HEARD
"I love you like a brother."	"I hereby reject your manhood with six words."
"Nothing's wrong!"	"Nothing is wrong. Everything's great. Let's watch football!"
"Does my butt look big in these?"	Danger! Danger! You can't win! Don't answer this! Run away!
"Fine! Go out with your friends!"	"It's okay, honey. Have a great time. I'll be right here whenever you're ready. Maybe I'll bake a pie."
"So where do you see this going?"	"Just exactly when are you going to commit, buy a ring, talk to my dad, walk down the aisle, and give up your freedom?"

GENDER BENDERS

Here's a little insight into the sometimes strange behavior of the opposite sex. See if you can answer the following questions. [And since we know you'll be confused, we'll give you the answers, too.]

Q: Why do girls go to the bathroom en masse?

[a] To talk about someone else at the table.
[b] To analyze how the evening is going and decode any hidden messages in looks exchanged or tones perceived.
[c] Girl A needs to borrow something of the feminine nature from Girl B, C, or D.
[d] All of the above.

A: [d] Any or all of the above at any given time.

Q: Why don't guys ask girls out more often?

[a] Fear that she'll say no.
[b] Fear that she'll say yes.
[c] Commitment phobia.
[d] All of the above.

A: [d] Any or all of the above at any given time.

Brain Drain

✳ If "e-lation" is the state of being incredibly happy, what is "re-lation"? Being happy *again*?

✳ Ever noticed that it's usually the guy who asks a girl to go *out*, but it's the girl who asks the guy to come *in*? Hmm. Interesting. Kind of interesting, anyway. Okay . . . maybe just a little interesting.

✳ Where did the concept of "hooking up" come from? You hook up a trailer to a pickup truck, a garden hose to a spigot, speakers to a sound system, and computers to a network. Think about it.

✳ Miss Piggy only kissed one frog and found her prince. Kermit only gave one pig a chance and found his princess. Lesson: Is there a green, slimy man in your life who deserves a second look? How 'bout a big ugly hog who has a really great personality?

✳ Ever noticed how many love songs there are on the radio? Where are the hate songs? There are some, to be sure, but not nearly as many. Why? Because love makes you feel like singing. And not-love makes you want to cut someone's throat out. That's why.

The Last Game

Here are a few games people play in an effort to capture the attentions of their hunk or hottie:

The Hard-to-Get Psycho Game

Have you been out there on the dating playing field lately? There is really no need whatsoever to pretend. Dates *are* hard to get—do we really need to make it any worse? Lame.

The Manipulate Shuffle

These people work frantically to be sure they "bump into" their potential flame in seemingly random places. They plan ahead on where to stand in line or sit at dinner, the movies, or church so they can be near the object of their affection. Manipulating situations at every turn? Lamer.

Whose Line Is It Anyway?

Whatever the other person likes, they suddenly like, too. You know those girls who pretend to like football, camping, and *Star Wars*? Or those guys who act like they enjoy chick flicks just because they're with you? The lamest.

[Legal disclaimer: Some genuine girls and guys may really share the aforementioned interests.]

So You Like Her?
Make Your Intentions Known

One of the most common complaints girls have in their pre-dating phase with a guy is the confusion they feel from perceived mixed signals. It may be because you don't know if you like her or not, and that's understandable. But if you do like her, and if you *really* like her, make it known. Here's how:

DO: Offer her your jacket, sweater, shirt, or dirty towel. Any article of your clothing on her person is like a canine "marking" a tree. Go ahead . . . claim her as your territory!

DO NOT: Talk to or flirt with everyone else in the room except her with delusions that she'll think you're popular and mysterious. It will backfire faster than you can say, "I'm a loser."

DO: Ask the girl out! She'll certainly get the picture then.

DO NOT: Have a friend, e-mail, text message, or answering machine ask her out for you. [Note: Girls, do not go out with a guy who uses one of these methods for your first date.]

DID YOU KNOW singles tend to sleep better? A recent study by Tylenol PM found that 60 percent of unmarried people get seven or more hours of sleep a night, whereas only 23 percent of married people got as much shut eye.

DID YOU KNOW that most single women factor in the Bling-Bling? A recent survey by *Jane* Magazine found that 62 percent of respondents said the size of a future husband's bank account does matter.

So You Like Him?
Make Your Intentions Known

If guys are bad about sending mixed signals, girls may be worse. You may find that you truly do like him one day and not the next, but then change your mind again the next day. Hey, that's cool. But if you like him, if you *really* like him, make it known! Here's how:

DO: Bake him something. It may sound old-fashioned, and it certainly sounds like work, but it will communicate your message for sure: "Cookies are sweet, and so am I, baby!"

DO NOT: Wear your heart on your sleeve. When you care what that certain guy thinks, sometimes the things he says and does [or *doesn't* say and *doesn't* do] can affect you more than if someone else said or did the same thing. Don't be overly sensitive; just be yourself and have fun. He'll like you more that way.

DO: Provide nonverbal cues. It's a fact that men respond to what they can see and touch while women respond to words and actions. So use that to your advantage—within lines of reason and purity. A simple pat on the shoulder or squeeze of the arm can speak volumes.

DO NOT: Stalk the poor guy. If it's meant to be, it will be, so lay off the manipulation game.

Surefire Signs You're in Love

You know you're in love when . . .

_____You smile, hum, daydream, and space out more than ever before.

_____You can't imagine ever facing one day without seeing the face of your significant other.

_____Cheesy love songs on the radio don't seem quite as cheesy somehow.

_____You're suddenly interested in the love stories of your parents, grandparents, mentors, and other people you look up to.

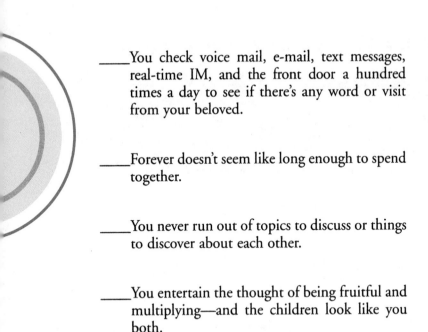

_____You check voice mail, e-mail, text messages, real-time IM, and the front door a hundred times a day to see if there's any word or visit from your beloved.

_____Forever doesn't seem like long enough to spend together.

_____You never run out of topics to discuss or things to discover about each other.

_____You entertain the thought of being fruitful and multiplying—and the children look like you both.

_____You are suddenly motivated to save money for a ring, honeymoon, or house.

SOUL MATE—FACT OR FICTION?

Main Entry: **soul mate**, *noun*
1: a person temperamentally suited to another
—Merriam-Webster Online [http://www.m-w.com/dictionary.htm]

In a very unscientific poll, not-so-scientific sources have found that an overwhelming number of people who are hopelessly single doubt the existence of true soul mates, while the majority of happily dating or newly married couples believe wholeheartedly in the sovereign plan that there is one soul mate for each soul created. Go figure.

SOLO STATS

A survey of 11,000 unmarried people by Yahoo Personals found:

- 70 percent of single females and 55 percent of single males agree that boxers beat briefs every time.
- 94 percent of singles agree that having a significant other who makes you laugh is important.
- 44 percent of men say they prefer a woman in black on the first date.
- 47 percent of singles say their hair was brown (instead of blond) when they had the most fun in their love life.

DID YOU KNOW that being single may actually help keep you skinnier? A recent study at Cornell University found that singles gained less weight than married couples over a ten-year period. In fact, it's estimated that women gain five to eight pounds in the first two years after walking down the aisle.

How Far Is Too Far?

[AKA: What Can I Get Away With?]

Hopefully by now, you've made up your mind already about how far you will allow yourself or your significant other to push the limits on purity. When "the moment's right and the moon is bright" is not the best time to trust yourself with big decisions like that! But you are human, after all, so here are some quick questions to ask yourself when things get steamy:

Would I mind if my grandparents were watching this? [This does not apply to grandparents who have severe cataracts and are legally blind.]

Are all my clothes still on?

Would I want my children to act this way? [Not with each other, of course. Yuck.]

Are all my date's clothes still on?

If my date were under 18, could I get arrested for this?

The Fast and the Furious

You know the moment. You're going 80 mph in a 55 mph speed zone—only you aren't behind the wheel; you're with your date.

What happens when you know you're about to go too far? First know this—time is critical! You only have a few fleeting moments of opportunity before those last rational warning thoughts are melted away by unbridled passion. You must act fast. Consider these surefire mood killers to pack in your arsenal for such occasions:

Laugh really loud.

Go to the bathroom and stay there a really long time.

Begin picking your nose.

Say, "Ouch!" really loud every 15 seconds.

Run like the wind! You can explain later.

Pretend you're making out with Weird Al Yankovic.

Fart, burp, or do both.

Or, if you're fresh out of bodily gases, just make the noise.

DIAGNOSIS: COMMITMENT PHOBIA

Main Entry: **com·mit·ment**
Pronunciation: kuh-'mit-muhnt
Function: *noun*

1 a: an act of committing to a charge or trust: as [1] : a consignment to a penal or mental institution [2] : an act of referring a matter to a legislative committee
2 a: an agreement or pledge to do something in the future; *especially:* an engagement to assume a financial obligation at a future date **b:** something pledged **c:** the state or an instance of being obligated or emotionally impelled <a *commitment* to a cause>
—Merriam-Webster Online [http://www.m-w.com/dictionary.htm]

Commitment phobia = the fear of commitment

EARLY WARNING SIGNS
OF COMMITMENT PHOBIA

✳ You score more rebounds than Michael Jordan ever did.

✳ The only way you can see yourself committed is in a white, padded room sporting a straitjacket.

✳ Your idea of true commitment is letting your latest relationship share in the experience of your bodily air releases. [That's "flatulence" for you proper girly girls.]

✳ You measure anniversaries in weeks, days, or hours.

✳ Whenever someone mentions a future together, you suddenly get sweaty palms and fuzzy vision.

Alternative Versions of the DTR

You've probably obsessed over this burning question at one time or another: *Where is this relationship headed?* And you duck and dodge the issue as soon as it enters the cognitive zone. First of all, you reason, who wants to bring that up now when things are going so well? And besides, what if you don't like the answer?

The age-old Define The Relationship [DTR] talk spans the decades and is responsible for much of the anxiety that consumes the planet. There has to be a better way to figure things out! So the next time you find yourself needing some clarity on your partner's intentions, try these alternatives and see if you don't arrive at the same place but with a little less stress.

Which do you like better . . . sprints or marathons? Bumper cars or go-carts? Diamonds or pearls? Roses or daisies?

If our life together were a Super Bowl, do you think we'd currently be in the play-offs, first half, fourth quarter, overtime, or victory party?

If we were on a road trip, relationally speaking, what might be next on our map? Rest stop? Refuel? New car shopping? Repair center? Two-car garage in the 'burbs?

Five years from now, if we were sitting here in this same place, would we both still have the same last names? [Okay, this one's not so subtle . . . On second thought, only ask this one if you're either trying to kill the relationship or propose.]

THE PERFECT STORM

Here is a list of questions and comments that are guaranteed to pick a fight, make someone really mad, and potentially kick off World War III:

FOR HER:

Are you gaining weight?
My mother never did it that way!
Why can't you be more like Nick's girlfriend?
Is it that time of the month for you or something?

FOR HIM:

Is your hair thinning?
You love your friends [or football team or dog] more than me!
Why didn't you send me flowers?
Wimp!

You've Lost That Loving Feeling

Here are five sure signs that a relationship is nearing the end
[or it should be]:

* The only eye contact you get is the one you insert for better vision.

* He needs more space than Neil Armstrong.

* Your friends refuse to say her name, using "your girlfriend" instead . . . even when she's in the room.

* He changed his home and cell numbers without telling you.

* She clings to you tighter than Saran Wrap.

. . . Or Is It?

Some of the all-time, dirty-dog, rotten, lower-than-low, scoundrel ways to break someone's heart:

* Cheat.

* Send a text message: Ran N-2 my X; C U later

* Take her to a theme park. After the roller coaster, hug her and say, "It's been a great ride."

* Hire a singing telegram.

* Keep repeating, "It's not you; it's me," nonstop, no matter what questions he asks.

* Tell her you've done genealogical research and found out that you're related.

* Show him a wedding ring and a photo of some children. [Your honey doesn't have to know it's your mom's ring and your brother's kids.]

* Make a compilation CD of all the breakup songs you can think of and mail it to her.

* Pack up all his stuff—and all your relationship memorabilia—and turn it into the airport lost-and-found.

* Say, "I'm sorry, but kissing you is like kissing my sister!"

* Tell him you never knew you were dating; you thought you were just "hanging out."

* Use the worst words in the history of relationships: "I hope we can still be friends."

* Ask her if she would mind if you asked out her roommate or her sister.

* Send a breakup e-card. [Try http://www.gottabreakup.com.]

* Announce it to him on the Jumbotron at a sporting event.

The All-time Best Advice
for Breaking Up

Be honest.

Keep it simple.

Don't string anyone along.
As soon as you know it's a no-go, cut and run.

When you actually break up,
do it quickly, like ripping off a Band-Aid.

Use "I" language and not "you" accusations.

Respect his/her feelings and ego.

Don't play games.

Don't call for at least two weeks afterward.
No matter what.

Return all borrowed items immediately.

Don't try to win over your ex's friends
or get them involved in any way.

Dating Blind

It's inevitable. Whether it's your mom, your aunt, your neighbor, or your long-lost cousin three times removed, everyone seems to know someone who would be just perfect for you. So what if they have a mullet, fangs for teeth, and funky body odor?

The next time you find yourself on a blind date, here are a few tips for surviving the setup:

❋ Only agree to go on a blind date that is set up by close friends you trust and who know you and the other person *both* well. [And even then, use caution!]

❋ Keep an open mind. Realize the situation is just as awkward for your date as it is for you.

❋ Never ever, no matter what, let your facial expression show disappointment or overexuberance at introduction.

✳ Dress comfortably. There's nothing worse than watching a stranger tug at their clothes all night.

✳ Never choose a messy dinner like ribs or spaghetti.

✳ The circumstances naturally lead to questions and answers about each other. Don't be shy about asking about things that matter to you. What have you got to lose?

✳ Allow destiny to take its course. If it's not working out, you'll both know soon enough.

✳ Remember that countless numbers of great love stories have started with blind dates.

LONELINESS BUSTERS

When the blues come calling, don't sit at home with double-Dutch chocolate ice cream or a six-pack of something you'll regret later. Get out there and do something instead!

Exercise. The chemical reaction in your body will help you feel euphoric and happy. And afterward you'll feel better about yourself for making such a good choice.

People watch. Take a shower. Do your hair. Paint your nails or shave your shadow, and take off to the nearest mall, airport, or playground. Pretend you're Forrest Gump and just sit and watch others. Have fun imagining what they're really like.

Phone home. There are plenty of people in your life who love you and would be ecstatic to get an unexpected call from you. Make the conversation all about them. It will let them know you care *and* get your mind off your own circumstances.

Volunteer. Oftentimes, the very best way to conquer the temptation to despair is to go out and do something nice for someone less fortunate. Focus on others, and your worries will suddenly seem a little less overwhelming.

Pick-up Lines
for Every Occasion

"How you doin'?" That's all Joey from *Friends* had to say to get a date. But if it's a little more difficult for you, here are a few pick-up lines that just might work:

"You must be from Tennessee. After all, you're the only *10-I-See!*"

"You look just like my first spouse."
  "Oh? How many times have you been married?"
  "None yet."

"God just told me you're the one!"

"Do you have plans for the next few months?"

"You're eyes light up this room like a couple of citronella candles on a redwood deck."

"Can I borrow your cell phone? My mom said to call her when I found the girl of my dreams."

"Are your feet tired? They should be, 'cause you've been running through my mind all night long!"

"Wanna enter my private chat room?"

"Have you been working out? I can see *us* working out!"

Popular Conversation Starters

MOST COMMON CONVERSATION STARTERS
IN COLLEGE:

What's your name?
Where are you from?
What's your major?

MOST COMMON CONVERSATION STARTERS
AFTER COLLEGE:

What's your name?
What do you do?
Do you like it?

Advice You Didn't Ask For
But We'll Give You Anyway
on Speed Dating

Honestly now . . . what on earth is your hurry? If this is the man or woman you are meant to be with for the rest of your life, do you think he or she will just magically disappear if you take things too slowly? Of course not! Take three deep breaths, two chill pills, one very cold shower, and enjoy the beginning of your budding relationship! Like Grandma always said, "Haste makes waste."

Oh, What a Tangled World Wide Web We Weave . . .

The popularity of online matchmaking continues to soar. In keeping with reality television dating, singletons looking for love are introduced to a number of different potentials and get to know them all simultaneously. You could be communicating with dozens at once. So if you take this route on the fast lane to anonymous love, be careful not to confuse all those soul mate wannabes. Here are some of the most popular sites:

```
eharmony.com
ChristianCafe.com
match.com
elovebug.com
```

FYI

If you Google "matchmaking," you will have more than 2.5 million sites to explore. "Christian matchmaking" narrows it down to about half a million.

DID YOU KNOW that the just about everyone gets married? It's estimated that 90 percent of Americans are married at some point in their lives.

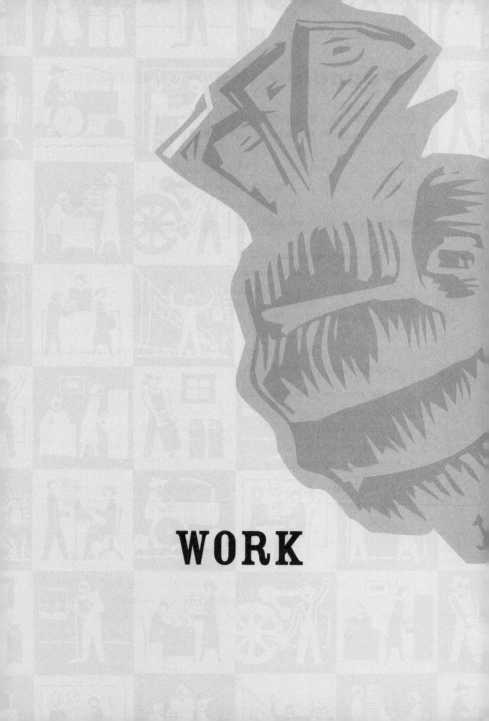

WORK

Pounding the Pavement

Finding a good-paying job can be rough. Unless you want to flip burgers or sell trinkets to tourists, you had better have a college degree, family members who own a successful business, or the last name "Hilton" or "Ritchie" and the connections to star in your own surreal television show. If you don't have any of the above, then you're going to have to roll up your sleeves and start searching.

If you've already tried the traditional route of scouring the local newspaper, here are some more guerilla tactics to landing a great job:

1. **Call your long-lost uncle.** The good old buddy of your parents. An old friend. Even if it's a second cousin twice removed, it's worth a phone call—especially if he or she has a successful business or lots of experience.

2. **Go online.** That's right. Join job groups online. Let other people be your eyes and ears. You never know who may spot a job for you. While you're at it, post those résumés all over the place. Just make sure the résumé is really good and has no typos.

3. **Get a makeover.** We're not talking Glamour Shots here. Just drive down to the hair salon for a trim. Go to the gym. Buy a new outfit so when those job interviews start rolling in you'll look and feel your best. You want that first impression to be a good one, so keep the body piercings and mohawk hidden unless you're applying for a job managing a Hot Tropic in the mall.

4. **Avoid selling door-to-door.** One of the biggest temptations while you're waiting for the big break is to start selling vacuums, magazine subscriptions, or an assortment of other for-only-247-easy-payments products. Don't trick yourself. It's not a step up from McDonald's.

5. **Keep an open mind.** Don't lock yourself into the idea of having one job or a particular job title. Rumor has it that Pringles has full-time potato chip testers and Club Med is always looking for employees. There are a zillion cool jobs out there that you probably don't know exist, so don't limit your search before you really start.

RÉSUMÉS PART I

If you ever want to buy a [fill in the blank], then you need a job. If you want a job, then you need a résumé. And it's got all the trappings of *which came first—the job or the résumé?*

When you make a list of all the jobs you've had since birth until now, you'll probably be depressed. It doesn't look like much compared to the forty-five-year-old who has twenty-plus years of experience and is battling for the same job. So skip the Prozac moment and get creative.

How can you rework your current and previous job titles into something with a little more flair? Here are a few examples:

Actual Title	Résumé-ready Title
Paperboy	Subscription delivery personnel
Grocery store bagger	Domestic product handler
Dog walker	Animal care specialist/supervisor
Gofer	Administrative assistant
Secretary	Executive assistant
Stay-at-home parent	Domestic engineer
Sales clerk	Customer service representative

Think big. Use words that have more than six letters. Before you know it, you'll be a professional—or at least sound like one.

RÉSUMÉS PART II

Once you've come up with great job titles, it's time to describe what your responsibilities were in those positions. Remember that you want to phrase your experiences in a way that demonstrates your value to your previous employer. Just make sure you aren't making stuff up.

There are some scary statistics that document the number of people lying on their résumés—you don't want to be one of those people. Your integrity is one thing that you can control, so make sure you are truthful in what you put down on paper or mention during an interview.

If you worked at McDonald's as an assistant manager, you may be able to say:

Managed and led teams of employees to meet or exceed customer requirements within a time-sensitive environment.

If you're computer savvy and frequently help fellow employees, you could say:

Helped train an ethnically and educationally diverse workforce in using various computer programs.

If you assisted your boss in balancing the books, you can claim:

Compiled in-house and client billing hours on a frequent basis.

The key is to combine an active verb [managed, trained, compiled, executed, maintained, etc.] with your duties. That's how scooping dog poop can become "maintained excellent sanitation standards" and spending a summer as an outdoor adventure camp counselor can become "organized activities and entertainment for young adults."

Your first and second résumé probably won't land you a CEO title or even a corner office, but if you're smart, you'll be able to leverage the experience you gained in your first few jobs to make your résumé a work of art and land that dream job.

`Moral of the Story:` If you do your best, work hard, and prove that you are willing to try new things while keeping a smile on your face, your résumé will start growing all on its own. It won't write itself, though, so keep the following in mind:

❋ **Keep track of every job you have ever had.** This includes your boss's name and contact information, your responsibilities, the amount of money you made, and the dates you were employed. If you ever received a raise or an award, you'll want to keep that information handy. You'll end up needing this kind of information at the strangest times, so make sure you keep it safe and plan on keeping it forever.

❋ **Make the most of what you have done.** Don't exaggerate or lie, but use the English language to your advantage. How you phrase things is just as important as what you are saying. Note the difference between "cleaning engineer" and "janitor"—which sounds more impressive?

❋ **Play it straight.** Avoid using colored paper, glitter, funky fonts, and outrageous print colors. Save all the pizzazz for decorating your apartment. If ever there was a time to lean toward the conservative side of design—good old black and white—this is it.

❋ **If you are struggling with your résumé, spend some money to sit down and meet with a career counselor.** Your state job center usually provides free counseling. These people are full of great information that can help you find a job you will enjoy.

DID YOU KNOW that The Donald has actually inspired a business class? Students at the University of Washington can sign up for Management Lessons from the New TV Hit: *The Apprentice.*

DID YOU KNOW that height really does matter? It's estimated that for every inch of height, your paycheck rises $789 a year. (*Cosmopolitan, June 2004*)

Recommendation Letters

Whether you're looking for your first job or your fiftieth job, a good letter of recommendation can go a long way. And a bad letter of recommendation can send you back to the land of minimum wage.

A letter of recommendation should include:

- The person's name and contact information
- Their relationship to you [A letter from your mom doesn't count. Nice try, though.]
- Why the person believes you were a good or, better yet, a great employee
- What your responsibilities were [But if they don't apply to the job you are applying for, these aren't necessary.]
- The person's signature

Once you get a good letter of recommendation, whether it is from an employer, teacher, or mentor, guard it, because it is worth its weight in gold. If you have proven yourself in other jobs, a prospective employer is more likely to take a chance that you won't go postal on their customers and give you a chance.

Once You Land the
Interview

It's your big day. You got a call back. You're gearing up for "The Interview." And you feel as if your entire future hangs in the balance.

Before you head out for your potentially life-changing morning or afternoon interview, you should have some questions about the company ready. Here are a few hints:

What would my daily responsibilities be?

Who should I go to for questions regarding pay, health benefits, etc.?

Is there any training that I can prepare for now before I actually start?

Always be ready to explain succinctly why you are the best person for the job. If necessary, write it down on a three-by-five card. Practice saying it to yourself and a friend. When you know your natural talents and can clearly express how you fit into a job situation, it shows you have self-confidence, did your homework, and really want the job. Those are three big pluses to an interviewer who is potentially going to talk to a number of other candidates that day.

THE STRAIGHT JACKET

If you're going to land a job, you have to look the part:

If you're in a corporate environment, buy some new suits. Think *The Apprentice* with Donald Trump.

If you're working for an airline, stick to the uniform.

If you're studying extraterrestrials in Nevada, go for the wild hair and stained lab coat.

Some Quick Tips:

✴ Unless yellow is *really* your color, leave it in the closet.

✴ Plaids and patterns don't dance. Avoid wearing them together.

✴ Avoid garage sales when shopping for your next power suit.

✴ Personal style is fine, but avoid fruity, wacky ties.

✴ For men, white T-shirts are a good investment. Buy them by the dozen.

✴ For women, only the devil really wears Prada. Buy some comfortable shoes.

Finding a Job
You Actually Like

If you're looking for a cool job, then go no further than www.coolworks.com. That's right, just as the name implies, this Web site offers cool jobs—from working in an island paradise to skiing some of the world's best powder, from Alaska to overseas. Your choices are limited only by your willingness to travel and your ability to get a passport. While the jobs generally don't pay very much, you'll be the envy of all your friends.

Picture this: They are in a suit and tie, living in a cubicle, and you are in a swimsuit and deck shoes on a white, sandy beach. You're now a screensaver on their desktop computer.

Combined with the awesome places you get to spend time in, you will meet people from all over the world and avoid the joys of interning, which usually include being handcuffed to a stapler or a copy machine.

Your Life as a Gofer

You might be wondering how a small, brown rodent relates to getting the job of your dreams. It doesn't—not at all. But there are times you're going to feel like a rodent told to go-fer this and go-fer that. During those moments, try to avoid screaming and running into the bathroom to find a happy place.

In case no one has told you, job descriptions rarely contain the word "gofer"; instead, it's disguised as "other duties as assigned." Look closely at your job description. It's probably in there somewhere.

Life as a gofer wears thin pretty fast. A few things to remember when you are on your fifteenth trip to the copy room before lunch to keep from going completely nuts:

✳ At least you have a job.

✳ It isn't much, but at least your boss tries to pretend that you're more important than you are by giving you a nicer title than gofer.

✳ You won't be a gofer forever.

✳ One day you'll have your own gofer. [Try to keep that malicious gleam out of your eye.]

✳ You might not have your own cubicle, but you are on a first-name basis with all the cute singles in the office.

✳ At least you won't have to battle the secretary spread [AKA weight gain] since you're always moving.

DON'T JOIN THE CROWD:
POPULAR PASSWORDS

You need a password for just about everything these days. So it's no wonder that the most popular password people choose is actually the word "password." You may think of yourself as a little more creative than that, but here's a list of other super common passwords. If yours in the list, then it's time to think of something new.

God

Love

Your birthday

The birthday of friends and family

Your name

The name of friends of and family

The name of your pet

Your address

Your zipcode

The same number multiple times, i.e. 999999 or 77777

A balance of numbers and letters, i.e. a1b2c3

A series of symbols, i.e. !@#$%

Ideally, your password should be at least six to eight characters long and mix letters and numerals. It should be changed every 4 to 6 months.

TAXES NEVER SEEMED LIKE A BIG DEAL TO US until we moved out of our parents' house. Up until that point, we didn't really care that a third of all the money we made went to the government. After all, between student loans and our parents' generosity, we were doing pretty well. We could afford junk food and a new CD or two every couple of weeks.

But when we started paying rent, buying our own food, and taking out small loans to pay for car insurance, our dislike of taxes jumped to the top of the list of concerns. Being young and naive, we decided that the workers in Human Resources [HR] would know where all the money was going. They mumbled some long explanation of the breakdown of why money was being subtracted from our checks. But after fifteen minutes or so, we realized that they didn't know either.

All we can figure out is that all those subtractions out of your paycheck add up to a few pluses like paved roads, public schools, care for the poor and elderly, and a long list of other items that may not always make you jump up and down for joy. We like the idea that part of our checks could pay for Grandma's medical care or feed a hungry kid. It might be forced generosity, but that's a lot better than a $500 toilet seat in Washington, D.C.

Bring Home the Bacon

CUBE LIFE

I have never had a corner office and I probably never will. Instead, I look around my desk and see a lot of prefab walls and cloth. I have tried to glam it up by putting up pictures, quotes, and other knickknacks, but it is still a cubicle. Occasionally I can look over the side of the cubicle beside mine for a view out of the window. But I can't usually see much.

The best way to approach a cubical is with grace, a plan, and some money spent wisely at Target. Recognizing that you work in a cubicle is the first step in getting help for a dreary work environment. Then it's time to take a proactive step and get organized. Develop a system that works for you. You may find an artistic arrangement of file folders works best. Or you may want to have dedicated "in" and "out" slots for your paperwork. You may be able to pillage the supply area and find some flashy pens, unusually shaped paper clips, or other office supplies that will help spur your creativity.

It's important to splurge with time and some money to make your cubicle your own. Invest in a cool clock or a hip lamp. Add some artwork and a few framed photos. Even if you change companies or cubicles, your goods can go with you.

As a side note, Dilbert isn't the most uplifting character to model your life after, but if you ever want to laugh about life in a cubicle—this guy can do it for you. Or just watch the movie *Office Space*, which will allow you to laugh out loud and decompress after a particularly stressful workweek.

DID YOU KNOW that young workers are switching jobs like crazy? According to the U.S. Bureau of Labor Statistics, the typical person holds 8.6 jobs between the ages of 18 and 32.

DID YOU KNOW young adults are entrepreneurial? A 2004 study by the National Association for the Self-Employed found that about 15 percent of its members are in their 20s or early 30s.

Trading Spaces

••

After being in school, having an entire cubicle as "yours" is quite a step up. At least it may seem like that for the first couple of weeks . . .

Of course, while you are still going through orientation and OJT [on-the-job training], you will have plenty of time to decorate with an eye toward sensibility, an expression of your personality, and comfort. So during your first week of work, you raid your photo albums and make frequent visits to business supply stores and the mall to pick up the following:

➤ Photos of graduation—*reminders that you really do belong here in the real world*

➤ Snapshots of friends and family—*these are the important people in your life*

➤ A bowl of potpourri—*the air seems a little stale*

➤ Fun little conversation starters—*these are cool little trolls with big hair, don't you think?*

➤ Special folders of different types of paper products—*you'll probably need a bunch of different paper for difficult projects*

➤ The coolest pens you can afford in every color made—*rubberized grip, gel rollerballs that write upside down in space*

➤ Post-it notes in every color and shape—*this way you can keep track of everything*

➤ A brand-new Rolodex—*for all the new people you'll be meeting*

➤ A great calendar with M. C. Escher prints—*pretty amazing how those steps keep going up!*

After decorating your new work space, then you can finally get down to changing the world with an out-of-date computer and rotary dial telephone.

And the weeks go by . . .

After ten weeks of work, you look around and realize that your cubicle seems to have shrunk. Ten weeks ago you remember measuring it for a rug that you never purchased and found that it was a very open and spacious eight feet by eight feet. Figuring that one of your coworkers is messing with you, you measure it again and it actually is the same eight by eight square. But something is different . . .

➤ You look around and recognize things are definitely different from when you started work.

➤ The photos of graduation have disappeared since you realized the folks around you aren't impressed by your *I've-never-heard-of-that-school-before* diploma.

➤ Snapshots of friends and family have been removed because there are some real weirdos in your office and you don't want to give them clues about where you live or those you love.

➤ The bowl of potpourri has been exchanged for numerous tree-shaped air fresheners since you can hang them around your neck, which helps you deal with the smelly guy in the next cubicle over who doesn't shower regularly.

➤ Those fun little conversation starters are in a desk drawer because you don't really want to talk to your coworkers unless you have to.

➤ All the special folders of different types of paper products have been given to your scrap-booking box because you haven't had a different project since you began working at the company months ago.

➤ The coolest pens you could afford have disappeared. They were on your desk when you left work Friday and were gone when you returned to the office Monday morning.

➤ The Post-it notes in every shape and color became an anniversary gift for your girlfriend since the only thing you need to remember for work is basic data entry.

➤ The Rolodex was helpful, at least for the box it came in. Putting your data entry spreadsheets on top of it has made your desk seem bigger.

➤ The great calendar with M.C. Escher prints has been replaced with a basic office calendar since your boss said that trying to figure out how the steps kept going up made him dizzy and you needed to take it home.

Oh well, you think. *That's my life in a cube.*

How to Avoid Going Postal

Your job is just that—a job. It's more than likely that you aren't finding a cure for cancer, AIDS, or poverty, but if you are, congrats. If you are one of those rare people who are volunteering full-time or living on rice in order to serve humanity, skip to the next section. You'll be just fine.

The truth is that nobody in your office would be there unless they were getting paid to be there. All who punched a time clock or filled out a time-card at The Company has made a decision to give X amount of hours of their life today so they can earn X amount of cash at the end of two weeks.

Wouldn't you love to be a fly on the wall of the corporate boardroom if the announcement was ever made that nobody would be getting paid on Friday? Any guesses as to how many cars would be leaving the parking lot early?

The secret to not going postal is recognizing that you might have emergencies, special projects, or reports that needed to be dealt with yesterday, but that these are still only work priorities, not life priorities. If you find yourself dreaming about your job at night or stressing over a work project while you're at the gym, then it's time for a priority check. You are not what you do.

As an employee, it is important to work hard and do your job well, but never at the expense of not having healthy relationships with God, friends, and family. If you are doing your job right [and your job description is truthful], then you should work hard for your employer 40 hours a week—maybe more if you are shooting for a raise or promotion or just need the OT [overtime]—and then spend the other 128 hours a week pursuing life. Not what our earthly boss considers life, but what our heavenly Father considers life.

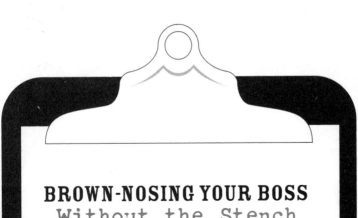

BROWN-NOSING YOUR BOSS
Without the Stench

Bet you thought you could actually brown-nose without being obvious, but guess what? You can't—so don't even try; it isn't worth the effort. Work hard, be yourself, and treat your boss the way you want to be treated. Nobody likes a brown-noser. You might be tolerated or humored, but you won't ever be liked or respected by your coworkers.

Are You the
Cream of the Crop
or Just Scum on the Top?

Integrity matters. Though everyone wants to succeed, you have a choice as to how you work toward that title, parking spot, or corner office. We all know people who have backstabbed, criticized, or bullied their way to the top. But without exception, these are some pretty miserable people. Since they aren't trustworthy themselves, they don't trust other people either, and that's a sorry way to live.

**Bosses who earn the
most respect usually do
the following:**

1. They do their best in difficult situations.

2. They take full responsibility
for their decisions—both good and bad.

3. They stand by their word.

4. They treat all of their employees
and their own boss with respect.

Integrity isn't something that just happens
when you get a promotion. It is something that is
learned and applied when no one is looking in the
break room or supply closet. Take the time now to
live your life honestly—you won't regret it.

Dealing with

Dips, Dorks, and Dudes

Coworkers can either make or break a job. No matter where you work, you are going to encounter some pretty strange ducks. You may be working with a clueless guy who makes inane comments at the weirdest times, a gal who wants to talk about nothing but hair care products, or a guy from Minnesota who grows his hair out, bleaches it blond, and tries to talk like a surfer when the nearest surf break is 400 miles away from your office.

Survival Tactics:

1. Know your own personality. Discover how neurotic you really are.

2. Ignore people. Unfortunately, this doesn't work very well, though it can be fun. No matter how hard you try to push the person's annoying attributes out of mind, the more you'll notice them. Eventually, you'll start getting upset over the littlest thing.

3. Try to create your own weirdness. Hum songs that stick in a person's head and never go away. Examples include "Ice Ice Baby" [from 90s wonder Vanilla Ice], "Follow the Yellow Brick Road" [from *The Wizard of Oz*], "(I've Had) The Time of My Life" [from *Dirty Dancing*], or "Killing Me Softly" [from *About a Boy*].

4. Lump yourself in the dips, dorks, and dudes category and decide to make the best of it. Try to find something that you can learn from all those oddballs. The great thing about this life is that regardless of what group of people you are most comfortable with, God will put people around you who cause you to rethink what you believe and even the way that you go about living life.

★ KNOW THYSELF ★

IN OTHER WORDS—GET TO KNOW YOURSELF!

Personality tests can help you discover how you respond to and react to other people. If you haven't taken a personality test, you should make time to take one. Your responses will help you identify your personality traits and how you interact with other people.

Start by taking free personality tests online in the comfort of your own home. Googling "free personality test" will yield countless options. Many of the free versions won't be as detailed as ones that you pay for, but this way you can start learning about yourself without dropping a wad of money.

If you have a close, trusted friend, you may want to share the results and ask for their honest feedback. Are the test results accurate? Which personality description best fits you? Allowing them to be honest with you will help you grow. They may point out something that is difficult to hear, but remember, that's why you asked them in the first place. You're already loved and appreciated just as you are or they wouldn't be your friend.

Personality tests have a way of popping the bubble of perfection that your mom spent years building up around you, but you'll be better for it. When you are able to recognize your strengths, you can start focusing your energy on an occupation or job that best suits you. At the same time, you can become aware of your weaknesses and how to deal with them rather than be surprised when they pop up.

"I like having employees who know what their strengths and weaknesses are. Whatever the work is, it always seems to flow better and people are able to operate in their areas of strength without making promises they aren't equipped to deliver on. That doesn't mean I don't assign people work that I know isn't their strong suit in order to challenge them, but it does make my expectations of them a bit more realistic."

—Personnel manager for the federal government

Wonderful things are possible if people are willing to step out on a limb and learn about themselves. Are you up to the challenge?

Pressin' the Flesh and Kissing Babies

Politics aren't limited to Washington, D.C. They are in every business, occupation, and work environment. Whether you like to play politics or not, you're going to have to learn to deal with difficult coworkers and learn to make friends with people who aren't necessarily your cup of tea.

The Rules of Office Politics Survival:

1. If you are asked to train the boss's son, do it well but start looking for another job.

2. Working with friends will get things done, and working with enemies is impossible. Don't hesitate to make things right; apologies work wonders.

3. If your boss is having a bad day, stay out of the way. Get your job done and give advice or a listening ear only if you have a good relationship and your boss has requested your insight in the past.

4. Want a raise? Ask your boss to schedule you into the calendar for a performance review. Even if you don't get a raise, you will be seen as a go-getter who wants to do a good job.

5. If a situation at work is keeping you up at night, start looking for new opportunities. Whether or not you can make the situation better depends on your willingness to persevere. Regardless

of whether you end up leaving your current job or not, at least knowing your options gives you some freedom and peace of mind.

6. Avoid office gossip like the plague. No matter what is said, no one comes out smelling like a rose. If you join the gossip-feeding frenzy, you'll end up having to apologize to a lot of people. Just say, "I've got to get back to work," and walk away.

7. Integrity and honesty are essential. Even if you end up looking bad, taking responsibility for your mistakes will keep office politics from ruling your life.

LIVING
ARRANGEMENTS

A BRIEF INTRODUCTION

Unless you are independently wealthy, have really generous parents, or are just really good with money, you are most likely going to have to get a roommate or two when you move out on your own.

Unless, of course, you prefer living in a cardboard box or self-storage shed without running water.

If you don't want to throw caution to the wind and put up a flyer at the local 7-Eleven telling anyone who stops in:

[a] **"I live alone," and**
[b] **"Here is my phone number. Call me sometime,"**

then you'll want to keep the advice in this entire section in mind.

Roommates 101

The General Rule: *Good roommates generally start out as friends or friends of friends.*

 You might not know whether your future roommate likes to clean, prefers to drink milk straight from the jug, or has personal hygiene issues, but if you or someone you know can vouch for their character, then the odds of your living with a raving lunatic drop dramatically. Knowing the person before you share living quarters is a good first step in avoiding the pitfalls of a really horrible roommate situation.

 If you're in need of a roommate, begin asking around. Talk to your friends, coworkers, and family members who live in the vicinity. See which names pop up. Remember to be patient. A few hundred dollars now spent in holding out for the right person can save you thousands of dollars in headaches later on.

 Granted, you may end up with a roommate who brags about their action figure collection 24/7 or someone who shouldn't have been allowed to leave their parents' house without a shock collar. We've had both. But even when we've had bad roommates, we've managed to live together without hurting each other, and in the end, our credit ratings weren't damaged too badly.

A REALLY BAD ROOMMATE

Love them or leave them—you'll always need them. Roommates are often the only way that you can afford a decent apartment when you first start out on your own. Sooner or later [and hopefully much later], you will probably have a bad roommate.

You'll finally have to draw the line. One of you needs to leave, and you'd prefer that your roommate do the packing. Of course, your roommate won't go willingly without a little prodding, so here are some ideas of what you can do to get rid of a really bad roommate. Don't rely on just one idea to scare your roommate off. Consider using a couple of these ideas at a time.

[Disclaimer: Any attempt to get a roommate to leave often means living in squalor and discomfort for a time. Using any of these ideas may result in visits by rental management, the Orkin Man, and other unsavory characters, including federal agents with handcuffs or lawyers with lawsuit papers, so proceed at your own risk.]

#1 The best way to get rid of a problem roommate is by sitting down and talking to the person directly. Be prepared to go over all the reasons you think the two of you shouldn't be living together anymore. When confronted with the negative things others think about them, most people will do whatever they can to remove themselves from the situation. Problem solved. However, if that doesn't work, here are 8 other options.

#2 Start setting your roommate up by making comments while watching gangster shows. Mention frequent trips that you used to make to various cities in the U.S. When you are both out to eat, visibly get upset anytime you can't sit with your back to the wall with a clear view of the exits. Wait until your roommate is gone for a day or more—change the locks and pay to have an alarm system installed. When they return, tell them that you were told by a friend from back in Chicago that your former employers heard that you were in the area and wanted to "talk" with you about early retirement.

#3 Start leaving food underneath your roommate's car to attract all the stray animals in the neighborhood. Once the critters are used to getting the food, start moving it around—from under the car to the roof and hood of the vehicle. When your roommate starts complaining about the scratches and having to wash his car frequently, point out that your car doesn't have that problem and suggest that maybe it is just that he has bad hygiene.

#4 Tell your roommate that you want to decorate the place a little. Go to Home Depot and buy a couple of houseplants on sale. Deliberately ask for plants that cause bug infestation problems. Also pick up some weather-stripping that you can apply to your bedroom door. When you get home, place the plants next to a window where the bugs will get plenty of light and warmth. Use the weather-stripping to create a tight seal around your bedroom door. Water the plants regularly and let nature take its course. Within a week, the living area of your apartment should be filled with swarms of little black bugs and your roommate's bedroom should be ready for a new tenant.

#5 This one will work as long as your roommate isn't a Goth or a fan of Marilyn Manson, though it will cost some serious money. Go to the closest mall and pick out an entire wardrobe and a black light from Hot Topic. Ask the salesperson for their advice regarding the best rave and underground thrash music they know of, and then go to the music store and pick up at least three of their recommendations. Go to Burlington Coat Factory and find the cheapest black trench coat you can find. When you get back to the apartment, move your speakers next to the wall closest to your roommate's room and crank up one of your new CDs. Turn out the lights in the bathroom and install the black light instead. After a week or so, you can up the stakes by starting a role-playing game at your apartment with a couple of new friends you meet in a comic-book store. If that doesn't send your roommate running for the nearest exit—then your roommate has some serious problems.

#6 This works best if your apartment complex is decorated with the thick, shaggy '70s carpet that frequently comes in shades of green or orange. Every time you buy bread, take the first end slice and tear it up into the smallest pieces you can. Sprinkle generously underneath your roommate's bed and in their closet. Cockroaches have the amazing ability to find the tiniest piece of food, and once your roommate starts thinking he is living in *Joe's Apartment,* it will be only a matter of time before he decides to move on.

#7 Everyone wants to be proud of their appearance and what people think of them. Roommates are no exception. You will have to get up before your roommate in order for this to work, but the early mornings are worth it. Take capsules of orange dye and put them inside the showerhead. When your room-mate gets up to take a shower before heading out the door, the water pressure will cause the capsules to break, leaving your roommate with an obvious carrot hue for the rest of the day. You don't want to do this particular trick every day because they might get suspicious. But if you set it up two or three times a week, you should get rid of your annoying roommate within a couple of weeks. It's a lengthy process but definitely worth the laughs you'll get from watching them go to work while trying to minimize their mandarin orange complexion.

#8 This one is a little gross but may be necessary, depending on your roommate's unwillingness to leave. If you are dating someone, don't forget to give the person a heads-up or you may be back on the single's circuit. The tactic is very simple—stop showering and using deodorant. When you start to really ripen, roll around on your roommate's bed, especially the area around the head of the bed. Put their pillows between your armpits and jog in place for half an hour. Then use their towel from the bathroom to dry the rest of you off. Even if they recognize that the bad B.O. is yours and call you on it, the fact that you were unclothed and rolling around on their bed should get them to consider finding a new place.

#9   Sabotage your roommate's dating relationship. This works for either a male or female roommate, but we'll use two male roommates as an example. Anytime you answer the phone and your roommate's girlfriend asks for him, ask for her name. When she tells you, make some comment that you thought that he was dating someone else, but it changes every week so who can keep track? This will set the ball rolling. He'll be upset, but you can plead ignorance. The next time she calls and asks for him, tell her that he gets upset when he talks to certain people and ask her if she is either Karen or Rebecca [assuming this isn't her name]. When she says, "No, this is . . . " reply, "Great, the last time one of them called, he was depressed for a week and started asking me to set him up on blind dates, but you aren't them, so hopefully it won't happen this time." Pass him the phone and let him know that the person sounds a little upset. After a few calls like this, your roommate will start looking for a new apartment—especially if it's a long distance relationship.

Now all you need to do is find another roommate who isn't a weirdo. Good luck!

The Multiplication of Roommates

Depending on your income level and the size of the place you live in, you may calculate that you need another roommate or two. The upside is that the amount of rent you pay goes down. The downside is that so does your quality of life.

```
1 bathroom + 2 bedrooms
  divided by 4 roommates
= Lack of Privacy
```

Having more roommates than bathrooms gives you a brief glimpse of what it will be like to be married someday and have all of your personal toiletry items jammed into one small corner of a counter [probably in an old black toiletry bag]. But it isn't just the lack of space that can get to you; it's the complete lack of privacy.

So as soon as you can afford a place with fewer roommates, even if it's a little smaller, make a move. And until you do, remember to establish boundaries. Let your roommates know what's okay and what's not so okay with you. And no matter what happens, make sure you set your foot down as to how your toothbrush can be used. Walking in on a roommate cleaning the toilet with your toothbrush might get him props for trying to clean, but it's still extremely gross. Set some boundaries and stick to 'em.

DID YOU KNOW that moving into an apartment can cost you a small fortune? David Morrison, president of Twentysomething, Inc., a young-adult research firm, told *Kiplinger* that he estimates the average apartment set-up cost to be close to $4,000. That assumes the new householder will shell out the first and last months' rent, plus a security deposit.

Common Bathroom and No Locks

Leif: The bathroom in my parents' house was the only door in the house that locked from the inside. For this reason, the bathroom became the sanctuary and was dubbed "The Library." The Library became the most desirable room in the house as my brothers and I grew up because it was the only place we could go and be by ourselves without the threat of interruption. We frequently ended up in brawls because we would race after dinner to lay claim to this favorite hideout.

Margaret: Growing up I didn't have to share a bathroom with a brother or sister [because I don't have any]. I had to share one with my parents! I remember getting told to "hurry up" a whole lot. Now I think I've figured out why.

Besides college, when I lived in a dorm and shared a bathroom with fifteen other girls, I haven't had to share a bathroom. Good thing. I don't think I'd be very good at it. Those white spots on the mirror always gross me out.

Leif: I've lived with dozens of roommates, and no matter what place we rented, I always ended up sharing a bathroom either with another roommate or with every visitor who came to the house. What was once my sanctuary became frequently intruded on by mere strangers. I couldn't just disappear into the bathroom for a couple of hours with a good book, because someone else always wanted to use it. And the lack of locks on the doors led to a number of rather embarrassing encounters with visitors to the apartment.

So to help others who might share in such bathroom woes, here is my list of ten ways to keep people out of a common bathroom that doesn't have locks:

✳ *Number 10*—Whistle or talk loudly to yourself anytime you have to use the restroom. [Not for use in public bathrooms.]

✳ *Number 9*—Two words: bungee cord.

✳ *Number 8*—Fix the doorknob so it only works from the inside. [Caution: Could be dangerous late at night.]

✳ *Number 7*—Carry your own "We're closed. Be back in . . ." sign for the door.

✳ *Number 6*—Every time you want some privacy, announce loudly, "I've got to go Number 2," and proceed into the bathroom.

✳ *Number 5*—Stop cleaning for a month or so and let the green mold creep out from under the door.

✳ *Number 4*—Hang a large "Occupied" sign at eye level whenever you head into the bathroom.

✳ *Number 3*—Install a fake video camera with a battery-powered blinking red light on the bathroom wall across from the toilet with a sign out on the door stating, "Premises are under video surveillance."

✳ *Number 2*—Stink bombs [both natural and manmade] are excellent.

And the Number 1 way to keep people out of your bathroom is [drumroll, please]:

Forget modesty and just leave the door open!

Margaret: Only with same-sex visitors, please!

Leif: None of these will work every time, especially with people who really need to use the restroom, so be prepared to combine as many of these as required to keep people out of your personal "library" or whatever you call it.

DID YOU KNOW a home might be on your horizon? According to Alliance & Leicester's movingimproving index, one in five people aged 20 to 29 are hoping to buy a property within the next two years, the highest percentage for any age group. (Taken from: http://www. findaproperty.com/cgi-bin/story.pl?storyid=6654)

YOUR STUFF VS. MY STUFF

Now here's an interesting dilemma: You and your roommate both have stuff—cleaning stuff, furniture stuff, and miscellaneous stuff. Whose stuff gets put in the closet and whose stuff gets used? No matter what you decide, you can't really win. Here's why:

1st—If you graciously allow your things to get put in the closet, you'll end up breaking something and having to give your roommate some of your cooler stuff.

2nd—If you decide to let your roommates use some of your stuff, not only will things end up being broken, but they'll replace your name-brand item with something from Wal-Mart. It's not fair, but unless you want to bring it to Judge Judy in small claims court, you are stuck.

Your best bet, which will only work with a roommate you don't already know, is to hide all of your stuff at your parents' house. Act like you're stuff-less. Even if you have to provide furniture, dishes, or a TV, you'll be able to shop at the Salvation Army. Then when something breaks, you'll know it didn't cost you an arm and a leg.

Branded or Open-range
Milk Containers

Food can become a major issue between roommates. It can polarize people more quickly than mentioning that you're a fan of Rush Limbaugh or Michael Moore.

Basic Rule: **Roommates who make more money than you will eat better than you. Roommates who make less money than you will eat worse than you.**

There are always exceptions to the aforementioned rule, but generally, more prosperous roommates will enjoy meat, vegetables, and cereal in a box, while the less fortunate roommates survive on Ramen, a bag of frozen mixed vegetables, and powdered milk.

It is always in the best interest of the less prosperous roommate to suggest that all of the food is shared. Initially, this is agreeable to most roommates since everyone wants to make a good impression. Unfortunately, once one roommate comes home to discover all the chicken breast and luncheon meats are gone, the days of the free meals will be over.

Shared food is similar to the concept of the free range back in the Wild West. Back before fences, everyone was prospering by allowing mixed herds of cattle to graze. In an ideal world, all of the roommates share the cost of decent meals. Unfortunately, neither the Wild West nor the idea of shared food exists today. Today we are left with branded cows and gallons of milk with your roommate's initials on them.

Branding doesn't just happen with milk, because over time, room-mates will start putting their mark on every type of food, beverage, and object that they have purchased. [Side note: If you or your room-mate brands toilet paper, it's gone too far].

All this branding raises the question: *Why is sharing so difficult?*

We've heard stories of roommates who have been able to share food amicably, but that's probably a myth, because we've never actually met one of these people in person. If you happen to be one of these people or know of someone who has actually experienced food sharing work-ing between roommates, we think that you owe it to the world to share your knowledge with others—start a Web site, a blog, something—you have important information that needs to be shared. Remember that with great knowledge comes great responsibility.

The Budget Gourmet
[5 Great Ways to Spice Up Top Ramen]

Number 1—Ramen spaghetti—Simply add your favorite spaghetti sauce to the cooked and drained noodles, heat, and enjoy. You can save the flavor packet for another recipe or special occasion. Also try adding some pepperoni slices and some Parmesan cheese, and you could call it Pizza Ramen for Monday night football.

Number 2—Spamen—While cooking the noodles with the pork flavor packet, cut up some chunks of Spam and toss them in. Once the noodles are cooked through, you are ready to go.

Number 3—Dry Ramen—This recipe still requires you to cook the noodles [without adding the packet of flavoring]. Then drain the noodles. Once they are sufficiently dry, put the noodles in the center of a large plate or bowl, and sprinkle the contents of the seasoning packet over the top. For a special treat, add a couple of cheese slices to the top and allow them to melt before digging in.

Number 4—I'm-too-lazy-to-even-boil-water Ramen—Break apart the noodles inside the original package. Take out the seasoning packet and sprinkle about half of the seasoning over the dry noodles and enjoy.

Number 5—Healthy Ramen—While you are waiting for the water to boil, grab a handful of mixed frozen vegetables. Throw them in the soup. You won't be lying to your mom that you're eating healthfully.

For additional Ramen recipes that are sure to make you cringe or lick your lips, check out Matt Fischer's Web site [http://www.mattfischer.com /ramen/]. He has over two hundred recipes that were submitted to him by Ramen connoisseurs from all over the world.

DID YOU KNOW your roommate might be ironing naked? According to a study by Niagara Spray Starch, 48 percent of 18- to 34-year-olds iron while naked or wearing only their underwear.

Biology Experiments You Can Do at Home

Leif: Did you know that in a hot, dry climate you can grow mold inside a sink basin up to six or seven inches deep? I didn't either until I came home from Christmas break to discover that my roommates had decided not to wash any dishes while I was gone. That's four roommates, each with their own set of dishes, left alone for nineteen days.

Close your eyes and visualize a double sink with cabinets two feet above the countertop filled with dishes from the top to the bottom. It was quite a sight [and smell].

The guys had decided that rather than clean the dishes as they got dirty, it would be easier just to wait for me to come home and take care of them. The day after I got back, I was so disgusted by the rotting food that I couldn't clean the dishes in the sink. I started washing them in the bathtub. I was doing fine until I got to the dishes that were inside the sink. That's when I discovered the mold. [Cue dark, forbidding music.] This wasn't your normal thin, filmy mold but a light, airy, fluffy mold like nothing I had ever seen before. The only way to describe it really is that it was like reaching into green cobwebs that the world's largest spider had spun. When I eventually got to the bottom of all of the stacks of dishes, I discovered that flies were hatching in the garbage disposal.

My roommates had created an in-house biology lab. I decided to create some boundaries. I do my dishes. They do theirs. Period. No exceptions.

Margaret: Boys are so gross! The only biology experiments that I've conducted have been in my car. I have a bad habit of carrying food in my car and having it spill out everywhere. [I'm not a very good driver, and I tend to take curves way too sharp, but that's another story.] Everything from milk to lasagna has made its appearance on my car's floorboards. But the absolute worst was when I spilled a half-gallon of Italian vegetable soup on the floor behind the driver's seat. When I went to remove the big pot of soup, it was sitting in an inch of Italian vegetable broth. I scooped out as much soup as I could from the carpeted floor and tried to clean up the mess. But within a week, a musty-smelling fuzz had begun to grow. I rented a wet-vacuum and went over the area again, but to this day whenever the floorboards get wet, the smell returns. It's a biology experiment worth skipping. So the next time you're traveling with food, make sure it has a sealed lid.

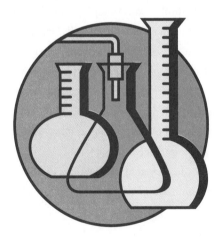

CAN YOU SAY "WINDEX"?

If you can say "Windex," especially in a roommate situation, then congratulations are in order—you are very special. Few roommates know how to say "Windex," let alone buy it or learn to use the little spray nozzle.

If you think about it, cleaning up after yourself, sweeping the floor, putting away the dishes, and taking out the trash really aren't difficult tasks.

Take five minutes and clean up around your apartment a little. The time away from the Xbox or your soap opera won't kill you, and even though your roommate might not ever notice, your significant other just might.

TEN SIGNS YOU'RE MOVING

1. Your car and home are littered with empty boxes.

2. You buy packing tape in bulk.

3. You have tuna fish salad and pickled beets for dinner in order to unload some canned goods.

4. You completely give up on cleaning.

5. The 116 little projects you've been putting off for the last 18 months are actually getting done or disposed of completely.

6. Every package you receive becomes a potential box for moving.

7. You realize you have too much stuff.

8. You wonder how you managed to collect all that stuff.

9. You promise yourself you're never going to collect this much stuff again (even though you know you're kidding yourself).

10. You have lots of people who offer to help you pack, but you politely say "no," knowing that you like to handle your own panties and per-sonals—thank you very much.

Adventures in Bill Paying

Just like in a romantic relationship, money can be a huge problem in the quest for a good roommate relationship. Whose name goes on the cable, Internet, electric, and water bills? Who is responsible for paying them? With everyone in an apartment having the cheapest checking account they can find and a maximum number of checks they can write a month, this can be a huge issue.

Online bill paying can come in handy in this situation, and you may find a gracious landlord who lets you pay with PayPal. If not, you're going to have to find a roommate who is willing to gather the money and pay the bills.

A few tips:

➤ *Appoint one highly responsible person to pay all of the bills.*

➤ *Appoint a second highly responsible person to gather all of the money from the others. If the same person has to gather the money and pay the bills, burnout is inevitable.*

➤ *Agree with your roommates to pay rent a few days early. This will prove helpful when your roommates write you a check a few days late. It will happen. Just wait.*

LIFE AT THE LAUNDROMAT
AND YOU'RE ALL OUT OF QUARTERS

One of the biggest hassles of living on your own is doing laundry. What a waste of time! But unless you want your clothes picked through by your nosy neighbors when you forget how long the dryer is going to take, you have to plan on spending two hours in a hot, muggy room with a bunch of people you will probably see on *COPS* in the next month.

Not only are laundromats full of interesting people, but most of the time, certain machines don't work. How many times have you scrimped and saved to have enough quarters to do laundry only to discover that the dryer you selected needs a new heating element?

We've discovered a new reason for premature hair loss: People pull out their hair at the laundromat.

Unless you have a small fortune in quarters to invest in laundromat testing [no animal should be harmed during these clinical trials], ask around to find the scoop on the best washer and dryer to use or at least be ready to bum some quarters from the guy picking his teeth with a knife and muttering to himself when you find out your clothes are still wet.

Reds and Whites Don't Mix

No matter how you mix a red sock and a white sock, the result is never pretty. You can try it with shirts, shorts, or sweaters, and the result will be the same—red and white clothes just don't mix. You'll end up with the strangest concoctions: a faded pink shirt or tie-dyed socks that promise to embarrass you in the gym. Whenever reds and whites meet in a load of laundry, you end up with clothes you really don't want to be seen wearing in public.

The solution is simple: Get two baskets for your clothes—one for darks and one for whites. Don't let them mix when you're doing laundry. If you do, you're going to end up with one of the sorriest wardrobes since the '80s.

DID YOU KNOW you may be able to afford more (or less) of a home than you think? To give you a general idea of what you can afford, triple your gross annual income. This figure assumes that you have 20 percent of the down payment and some student loan and car debt. Depending on these and other factors, you may be able to afford more or less of a home or condo.

Crashing at Home
[HI, I'M BACK WITH A DEGREE]

Fast Fact:
60 percent of college graduates plan to move back home after graduation.

You thought you were going to be out on your own, but you've decided that you'll take advantage of your parents' revolving door policy and reluctantly move home. If so, you're not alone. A surprising percentage of people in their early 30s are still living at home. Granted, you don't have to be one of them, but if you find yourself invading your parents' empty nest, here are a few guidelines to keep in mind.

Communication is key. After you move back into your old room, which may or may not have been converted into an office or sewing room while you were gone, you need to sit down and have a one-on-one with your parents. What are their expectations? Do you need to pay for rent? Contribute to food costs? Clean? Also, talk about your expectations.

Know the rules. Do your parents have rules or guidelines they expect you to live under? Do you still have a curfew or need to let them know where you're going? Do they feel they can dictate how you dress, who you hang out with, or what you do with your time? You need to know their rules before you can decide whether you can live under the same roof with them again.

Establish boundaries. Even if your mom is initially twitterpated about having you home, you still need to talk about how long you're going to stay. Develop a timeline in your mind, add three to six months, and make sure your parents are comfortable with that.

Set up a regular debriefing. Select a time—once a month or every few weeks—when you can get together with your parents and talk openly about what is and what isn't working.

RECLAIMING YOUR ROOM

If you have been away from home for any length of time and then decide to return, you'll discover there's truth to the old adage, "You can never go home again."

Leif: My parents actually sent me photos that documented the renovation [AKA destruction] of my childhood bedroom. The first photo showed a crowbar going into the wall. The last photo revealed the remains of my room being burned. My room was gone. I think my parents thought I would be happy about all the upgrades and renovations to the old homestead. Instead, I sulked thinking about how my bedroom had been forever changed.

Margaret: My parents were gracious enough to preserve my room after I graduated from college. Unfortunately, within a few years of receiving a diploma, they decided to sell the house and live on a boat. So now I don't have a room or a home I can claim as my own. It's kind of weird.

Leif: Maybe like me you've had to go through the traumatic experience of coming "home" to no room at all. The house might look the same on the outside, but on the inside everything is different. Your bedroom has changed, you've matured [hopefully], and your parents are over the empty nest and are ready to live like newlyweds again.

If you have to move back home again, for whatever reason, you may find it hard to make your old bedroom feel like your place. Whether Mom converted your room to her sewing area or Dad uses your room for his reloading equipment, it just may not seem the same. No matter what, be ready to roll with the changes and you should be able to handle the transition.

You Changed My Diapers.
CAN WE REALLY BE FRIENDS?

Leif: I never thought I would be shooting at my dad.

We don't belong to some Kool-Aid drinking cult, so I never thought it would come to this. Grown men out in the woods, fighting mosquitoes and shooting paint balls at each other—who'd have thunk it!

I'm truly out of the house now, hopefully for good, and my dad and I are actually friends. I can call him on a Saturday afternoon and he'll stop doing chores around the house to come and get covered with paint just so he can spend time with his son.

Now not every father is willing to endure pain and discomfort to spend time with his kids, but maybe your dad will sit and watch football on Monday night or take you to a NASCAR race. Go to garage sales with your mom. Cook meals together. Whatever you do, make an effort to spend time together. In any case, I recommend that you try to be friends with your folks. That doesn't mean you have to force yourself to spend time doing something you hate, but try to find things that you can do together and still have fun.

God gave us parents for a reason—some parents are bad and some are exceptional, like mine. But if we don't take the time to learn how to live life honoring the people who brought us into this world, we'll miss a pretty big part of God's plan. And you just might discover that they're smarter than you thought they were.

FRIENDSHIPS

The Friend Hunt

So you are in a new place, working at a new job, and don't know a soul where you live?

Congrats! You are officially going through one of the most challenging times in your life. The good news is that there are lots of people around you going through the exact same thing. You have two options:

[1] Stay as close to your apartment as you can. Convince yourself that you can be a monk and do everything you can to retreat from the outside world.

OR

[2] Hang out with coworkers from the office who remind you the most of the "popular" kids back in high school. The relationships will be deep and meaningful and help you figure out who you really are.

[Please note: The second option isn't even remotely true. If you really think that's the answer to the problem of loneliness, you need think about what it means to be a true friend.]

Finding people to spend time with is hard, but finding actual friends also takes diligence and a lot of effort. Start looking in a place where people with similar interests hang out. If you play racquetball, then hang out near the racquetball courts. If you like to read, hang out at the local coffee shop in town or volunteer at a library. If you love music, consider getting a part-time job in a music store. You will end up meeting people who have similar interests. They won't all end up being your BFF [best friend forever], but you just might have some cool new people to spend time with.

FORMING A TRIBE

[Unofficial] Definition—tribe: Your peeps. Your people. Your homies. Your gang. The people you can call to pick you up at the airport when you fly in at 2:00 A.M. The friends who will eat a pint of Ben & Jerry's with you after a breakup. The ones you call when you're at your best or your worst.

You've heard it said, "You are what you eat." Well, the same is true about your friendships: "You are who you hang out with." You can't let just anyone know the deep secrets of your heart. You have to pick wisely. Some people are worthy of a 4:00 A.M. confession about your past. Others are not. Those who make the cut can be members of your tribe.

A healthy tribe consists of a group of people who share common interests. You may share the same faith, an appreciation for the arts, or unity in a political cause. With a cornerstone belief system or set of interests that unites you, you can find people who you can live life with. Sure, there are topics you may disagree on, but you're willing to accept those differences with grace.

In a healthy tribe, you end up spending time with people who are different from you. You may have a nurse, accountant, teacher, architect, and three people who are still unemployed trying to figure out what the heck they're going to do with their lives in your tribe. But come the weekend, you're all hanging out, eating dinner, hiking, or enjoying a concert together.

Tribes, in essence, become a second family. They're the ones with whom you celebrate your birthdays, mourn your job loss, and veg out on a rainy Saturday afternoon.

The Influencer

Personality will play a role in any tribe, but the Influencer is, as the name implies, the most influential member of the group. It doesn't matter whether the person is male or female, the oldest or the youngest, boisterous or quiet, or anywhere in between— what that person does, the rest of the tribe does as well.

If that is the role you find yourself in, be aware that you have a lot of responsibility and can use your influence for good or evil. You are the silently elected role model. If you choose to buy tickets to a concert, everyone else is going to want to go. If you decide to make fun of someone, everyone else will agree. If you decide to do something to make a difference, like adopt a child with Compassion International, then everyone else will adopt one, too. Whether you like it or not, you're being watched. Your words and actions make a difference not only in the lives of your friends but in the lives of their friends as well.

If you want to be the Influencer, you probably aren't going to be. When influence is forced on people, it normally backfires, so be patient and wait on your turn to be the Influencer.

DID YOU KNOW you don't have to accidentally wake-up your best friend who is living in China or South Africa by calling at the wrong time? Simply visit www.timeanddate.com to find out what time and date it is anywhere in the world. You can even create your own clock to keep tabs on overseas friends.

CONVO TOPICS TO AVOID

(UNLESS MAYBE YOU'RE WITH YOUR BESTEST FRIENDS)

➤ Religion—If it comes up naturally, then speak naturally, but avoid any 3-point sermons, soap boxes, or anything that can't be spoken in love.

➤ Sex—Whether it's your bedroom or theirs, you can skip this slippery slope of a topic.

➤ Plastic Surgery—Surely you have an opinion, but the person you're talking to may have more than an opinion; they may had something done. So leave the Nip & Tuck to TV.

➤ Homosexuality—You may be tempted to rant about this one, but no matter what side you're on, the person you're with just might be on the other.

➤ **Abortion**—Like homosexuality, you're playing with fire if you jump into a heated debate on this topic.

➤ **Politics**—Leave the future of the red, white, and blue in someone else's hands

➤ **Parenting**—Whoa there! You may be willing to chime in on how so and so is raising their little ones, but unless you have something nice to say, don't say it at all. This topic is far more personal than you can ever imagine.

➤ **Size & Weight**—When it comes to weight, especially a woman's weight, run for the hills. Avoid at all costs. Mayday! Mayday!

➤ **Income**—What anyone is or isn't making in salary or bonuses is an obvious no-no.

➤ **Other People**—The old rule applies: If you can't say something nice, then it's probably best not to say it at all.

Realities of Community

Within a tribe of committed, caring, and compassionate friends, there will be plenty of opportunity to point out the negative and harass others about the inconsequential. But real community [AKA true friendship] comes after there has been a chance to stand together when things are bad, to rejoice as they get better, and to lend a hand in support when someone can't handle it on their own.

Consider the following:

* Who did you call the last time you didn't know who to talk to?

* Who naturally has a knack for knowing something is wrong before you ever tell them anything?

* Who is willing to reschedule their plans to be there for you when you really need them?

Those are your true friends. Those are the people you need to invest time in and make sure you take the time to support them in turn. Those are the people you can trust to have your best interests in mind. Those are the people you can trust when they encourage you to make a change in your life.

The reality of authentic community—real relationships with people—is that it's sometimes messy. Feelings get hurt. Mean things are said. Important details are forgotten. At the same time, authentic community allows for forgiveness to be offered, mercy to be extended, and relationships to be reconciled.

The reality of community is that everyone grows.

Signs of True Friendship

Here are some of the signs of true friendship. Remind you of anyone?

True friends:

- tell you when you have a yellow booger hanging out of your nose.

- gently pat your shoulder to wipe off the dandruff.

- offer you a mint or piece of gum when you truly need it.

- warn you that your new date has a bad reputation.

- hold you accountable to telling the truth.

- listen.

- are honest but gracious with you.

- challenge you to lead a life of integrity even in the little things.

- confront you when you are wrong.

➤ see you at your worst and encourage you to be your best.

➤ want to defend you when someone wrongs you.

➤ give and receive from you.

➤ defend you.

➤ don't drop you when something or someone better comes along.

➤ know the song in your heart and sing it back to you when you forget the words.

➤ encourage you when you're down, strengthen you when you're weak, and do all that other stuff you read about in Hallmark cards.

When you find someone who is a true friend, hang on to that relationship. You've found a treasure.

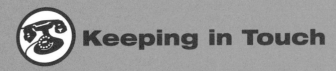# Keeping in Touch

In case no one has told you by now, you don't have to let great friendships go just because you move or are physically far apart. You can keep friendships alive for five, ten, even fifty years. But it's not going to happen without some diligent effort on your part and a bit of reciprocation from your friend.

Ways to keep a long-distance friendship alive:

Instant messages and e-mails. Your computer provides one of the cheapest, quickest ways to keep in touch with people. You can instant-message if a person is online at the same time, or use e-mail as a backup. Take an hour a week to write people you really care about. Instead of typing in the same story of how you almost ran over a goat twelve times, just cut and paste it into personalized messages. A little effort on your part will go a long way to keep your friendship strong.

Speed dial. Cell phone packages often come with bundles of night and weekend minutes. Use them to call people you care about. If you [or your roommate] don't have a cell phone, then invest in a calling card. Some are less than 4 cents a minute. That means you can talk for an hour for less than $3. That's better than a movie.

A good old-fashioned pen. When was the last time you received a handwritten letter or card? How did it make you feel? Make someone else feel that great by taking the time to write one of your own. You may want to take a pad of paper or set of cards with you on your next long flight or drive [assuming you're not behind the wheel]. You'll be amazed at how many people you can touch base with while traveling.

Care packages. Nothing says "I'm thinking of you" more than a four-day-old, semi-stale, nearly completely crushed batch of home-baked cookies from halfway across the country. Bake something fun. Buy a few treats. Run through the local dollar store with $10. Package up your presents and ship them off to someone who is going to have a brighter day because of you.

Postcards. They're cheap. They're cool. They're fun. And they don't require much writing. Whether or not you take a trip out of town or across the state line, pick up a few postcards and write some kind notes to friends. It doesn't take much to strengthen a friendship.

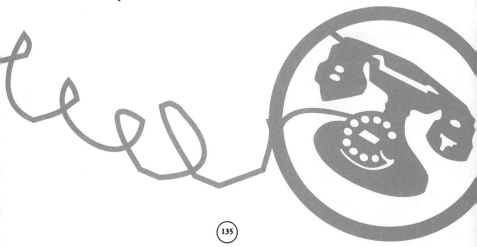

DID YOU KNOW some things about friendships never change? When 100 girls were polled by YM, "What's the most important quality in a best friend?" more than half said dependability, 20 percent said one who never lies, 9 percent said sense of humor and 5 percent said compassion. Those are good qualities in a friend at any age. (Source: YM, April 2000)

FRIEND MOVIES

The Lord of the Rings trilogy
The Fox and the Hound
Remember the Titans
Steel Magnolias
Garden State
First Wives Club
Scent of a Woman
When Harry Met Sally
Stand by Me
My Best Friend's Wedding
Then and Now
Batman and Robin
Thelma and Louise
Beaches

GOOD FRIENDSHIPS GONE WRONG

If you've ever experienced the loss of a solid friendship, one or more of the following probably contributed to the demise:

- Money matters
- Competition
- Time deprivation
- Self-interest
- Comparison

Bad Friendships Made Good

When things go wrong between friends, as they do from time to time, it doesn't have to be the end. A few basic concepts can save any friendship:

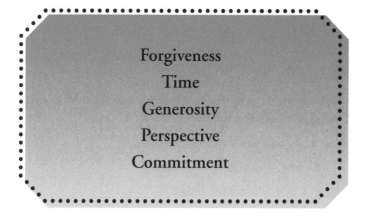

Forgiveness
Time
Generosity
Perspective
Commitment

Stuck-in-a-Rut
Relationships Revived

If you've been great friends forever, grown up together, and know everything there is to know about each other, you may be tempted to take your friendship for granted. Instead, add some spice to it. Make new memories. Try these for fun:

✳ Take a trip to somewhere neither of you has ever been.

✳ Read a book together.

✳ Cruise down memory lane with journals or photos. Make a list of all the greatest memories you have together.

✳ Start a new tradition. Be creative.

✳ Learn a new sport or hobby together.

✳ Set up a once-a-month lunch date.

✳ Call your friend the next time you need one.

✳ Write a personal letter expressing your appreciation of the friendship.

✳ Spend a day riding roller coasters together.

✳ Volunteer together.

How to Be
FRIENDS WITH GOD

Did you know that you can be friends with God? It may sound a little strange, but it's true. What does a relationship with God look like in real life? The truth is that it's pretty multifaceted. It includes sinner to savior, child to parent, employee to boss, beloved to lover, friend to friend . . . the list goes on.

Being friends with God may sound creepy or superspiritual to some. But it's really the same as any other friendship. To make it grow, you have to invest in it. Do a couple of these things and you will see your friendship grow:

1. Spend time together.

2. Talk. Listen. Don't only talk. Don't only listen.

3. Learn what he likes and doesn't like.

4. Give gifts [your time, your abilities].

5. Send a card [write in a prayer journal].

6. Read cards from him [Scripture].

7. Call on him when you need someone.

8. Be yourself. Be real.

9. Talk about him with mutual friends.

10. Introduce him to others.

10
Ways to
Tick God Off

1. Be mean to his kids.

2. Ignore him.

3. Ask him for stuff all the time. Take, take, take, and never give.

4. Use his name in vain.

5. Say one thing and do another.

6. Lead others astray.

7. Ask for his guidance and then do whatever you want without waiting for the answer.

8. Reject his Son.

9. Do a halfway, halfhearted job.

10. Perform the right duties with the wrong motivation.

THE
BLING-BLING

9 Easy Steps to
Establishing a Budget

You'll need:

A container to store receipts	Tissues [if you're emotional]
A pencil or pen	Ben & Jerry's [if you need comfort]
Small notebook	Desk or writing surface

1. Beginning on the first day of the next month, start putting all your receipts in an envelope, drawer, plastic baggie, or old shoe.

2. At the end of the month, divide your receipts into different piles, including:

Food, Transportation/Car Expenses, Rental/Home Expenses, Phone/Television, Clothes, Travel, Entertainment, Insurance, Eating Out, etc.

3. Add up the total of each pile. Record each total in your notebook.

4. Add up the total for all your expenses.

5. Compare your total expenses with your total income. Determine which is greater.

6. If your expenses are greater than your income, then it's time to either [a] cry like a baby, [b] console yourself with a tub of ice cream, [c] bang your head against your desk.

7. When you're done with that, it's time to look for ways to cut expenses. Where can you cut expenses that will have the least impact on your lifestyle? Can you downgrade your cell phone plan or cable programming? Can you take lunches to work or rent a movie with friends rather than go to the theater?

8. Once you've gotten your expenses below your income, move on to No. 9.

9. Ideally, you should be putting some of your extra money in an emergency fund. In a perfect world, you should have six months' income in the fund. But in the real world, it may end up being a lot less.

Stuff Your Paycheck Can't Cover

Lots of people drive nice cars, have bumpin' stereo systems, and wear great clothes, but they don't actually own any of it. Just because you swipe a card at a cash register and walk out the door with a new product without getting jumped by a mall cop doesn't mean that the stuff is actually yours.

Until you pay back the people who loaned you the money—*nothing is really yours.* Credit cards can be evil. They may be a necessary evil at times, but they like to take away any chance you have of getting ahead. Remember that unless you can make a purchase and pay it off at the end of the month, then you should probably learn to live without it for a little longer. Sure, your neighbor may have the newest iMac, but eventually you'll be living in a house and your neighbor will still be cramped into an efficiency apartment with an obsolete computer.

Rent, expenses, and your total bills are probably going to consume 85 to 95 percent of your income. The paltry 5 or 15 percent left over for entertainment, toys, and fashion isn't much, so you're going to have to buy wisely. It's worth your time to go online and look for counsel on how to spend or save this hard-earned cash.

When it comes to finally spending that dough, a magazine called *Consumer Reports* needs to become your new best friend. It is a wealth of knowledge. It will help you buy the best product for the money and steer you away from buying any lemons. If you don't want to subscribe without checking it out, visit your local library.

Like your time, money is also a precious commodity. Spend money on things that will last, because in the end, things will break or need repair and the money you spent on them will need to be earned again.

Good Debt vs. Bad Debt

It's pretty hard to avoid debt altogether. Let's face it. You can only ride a bike and live out of a tepee for so long. Sooner or later, you're going to want to upgrade your lifestyle, and that requires debt. Unless, of course, you're a trustafarian.

[DEFINTION] **Trust-a-far-ian: A person who has a trust or bank account, usually established by a wealthy family member, from which they receive payments or can draw amounts of money. Not related to a Rastafarian.**

[Taken from Margaret and Leif's Unofficial, Unpublished, Unwritten-except-for-this-one-entry Dictionary.]

So before you take a bigger plunge into debt, you need to know the difference between good debt and bad debt. Simply put:

Good debt helps you build your net worth or overall quality of life. Student loans are a prime example of good debt. They generally carry a lower interest rate and allow you to get an education, which increases your chances of landing a better job. A house can be considered a form of good debt. There's a good chance that your home will appreciate, and your house can serve as a way of saving money rather than just spending it on rent. As a bonus, you earn tax credits.

Bad debt reduces your net worth and overall quality of life. Credit cards are the most common form of bad debt. You often pay exorbitant interest on the items you purchase, so any savings from purchasing it on sale are eaten up by the extra payments. In the end, you can end up paying two or three times the original cost due to interest rates. Plus, you can't write off the interest.

In short, always pick good debt over bad debt. But the best choice is still to avoid debt of any kind whenever possible.

STUDENT LOANS:

Love 'Em or Hate 'Em,
YOU STILL GOTTA PAY 'EM

Fact: Approximately 64 percent of students graduated with student loan debt. The average student loan debt is $16,928.

Feeling the weight of your loans? Thumbing through your payment books and wondering why they're so stinkin' thick? You're far from alone.

While the interest on student loans is usually lower than other loans, it's still worth shopping around and talking to a loan consolidator to find out if you can get a better rate anywhere else. In the meantime, make double payments whenever possible.

And whatever you do, don't assume that just because you head to Tahiti they won't find you.

Keep your payments flowing, and for your credit records, also make sure they arrive on time.

DO YOU KNOW what your friends are bringing home? For those under 25, the average income before taxes is **$19,744.** ("The WWD List: The Age of Influence," WWD, August 29, 2992, 10).

PICKING A CREDIT CARD

Choosing a credit card is a lot like buying a new coat in the fall. There are so many to choose from. The goal is to find one that fits you and your personal style.

Basic Situation: Which credit cards do you qualify for? Depending on your job status, you may find have some pretty slim pickins. If you have a lot of debt and a limited income, then find the credit cards with the lowest possible interest rate and fewest fees. If you can't find one with a 12 percent interest or less, then you may want to avoid having one altogether.

Good Situation: If your post office box always seems to have one or two offers, then you may be able to land yourself a deal. Look for promotional offers, which include zero percent interest for the first six months. It may be possible to surf these credit card offers for a year or more. Ideally, though, you should still try to pay off your bill every month.

Great Situation: If your post office box is overflowing with offers and you're in a financial position in which you can know you can pay off your bill each month, then you can look for the perks. Credit card companies offer a variety of perks with money-back offers, frequent-flyer miles, and credits at name-brand vendors to name a few. Many of these perks require an annual fee as well as a higher interest rate if you can't pay off your bill in time.

DO YOU KNOW you're not the only one who has some questions about Social Security? A survey of 18-to 34-year-olds by Oppenheimer Funds found that 84 percent of respondents favor giving workers a choice of where to invest their Social Security taxes. Some 53 percent think they will outlive Social Security. (Elsa C. Arnett, "Generation X-ers Indifference Could Cost Them More Than They Think," Knight Ridder/Tribune News Service, January 27, 1999).

Climbing Out of the
Black Hole of Debt

DEBT BECOMES US.

Sounds like the opening line of a book. But really, debt does become us, if we're not careful. If you've found yourself in the black hole of debt, there are two pieces of good news: You're not alone, and it is possible to escape. But it's going to take three ingredients:

```
Discipline
Hard work
Sacrifice
```

Discipline means that you just can't have what you want exactly when you want it. It means waiting until you've paid off debt to buy something new. Now along the way, you can reward yourself. When you're able to pay off $1,000 or more of debt, allow yourself to splurge on something small you'll enjoy for all your hard work. Obviously, it isn't time to buy a new home entertainment system, or you'll be right back where you began.

Hard work means that you may need to get a second or third part-time job to pay off your debt. If your forty-hour-a-week job isn't bringing in enough green to get you ahead, then it's time to volunteer for overtime. If your boss isn't interested in your generous offer, than look at moonlighting at a second job. Take the extra income and pay off what you owe.

Sacrifice means that you can't always have what you want. If you take time to save, you can be debt-free and still drive a decent, trustworthy set of wheels. Or you can sign up for a loan and drive a new pimped-out vehicle. Just don't forget that you'll be carrying a load of debt in the backseat wherever you go. Getting out of debt, and more important, staying out of debt, requires making some sacrifices, simplifying, saying no, and making wise decisions with your resources. It's not always easy, but in the long run you'll end up way ahead. And if you save hard enough, you just might get to drive the pimped-out vehicle after all.

Short on Cash?

A rock concert. A nice dinner. Tickets to the ball game. The latest movie. A theatrical performance. An amusement park. A ski trip. Two rounds of golf.

Let's face it, fun can get pretty expensive.

Here are some ways to have fun when you're short on cash:

Take swing or salsa lessons

Picnic in a park

Run around a playground

Rent your favorite show on DVD

Go to an afternoon matinee

Plan a scavenger hunt

Attend a high school football game or play

Play board games

Host a snowball fight

Visit an art gallery

Watch the sunset

Feed the ducks

Rent your favorite movie

Go bowling

Visit your library for free movies, books, and entertainment

Cook a new dish

Play putt-putt

Volunteer

8
Things to Buy
WHEN YOU CAN AFFORD THEM

No. 1. Health insurance

No. 2. Wheels [preferably four]

No. 3. Laptop

No. 4. Clothes for a wedding, funeral, and job
interview [preferably not the same outfit]

No. 5. A day at the spa . . . or at least a massage
[Even you guys will enjoy this, trust us!]

No. 6. Durable, high-quality luggage

No. 7. Super Soakers and water grenades

No. 8. Professional briefcase or messenger bag
[Note: Never attend a job interview
sporting your old college backpack!]

No. 9. Dishes that match

No. 10. Real artwork

THE STASH OF CASH

You need a savings account. And it needs to have more than $200 in it. Even if that sounds like a lot, you need have a just-in-case fund. Because you never know when something crazy will happen:

* Like a herd of elephants stampedes your vehicle.

* A shoe thief robs you of all your footwear.

* You accidentally light your friend's couch on fire.

* Killer bees decide to take refuge in your house for three straight weeks.

* You twist your ankle while chasing a puppy through the park and need a doctor.

* Your roommate gets taken away in a straitjacket and you can't pay all the rent yourself.

Okay, maybe these are a little outlandish—with the exception of your friend's couch—but so are all the little things that can add up to big expenses. So every so often take a $5, $10, or $20 bill and stick it in an envelope for when something goes wrong. Just don't keep it in your freezer or underwear drawer—all the thieves know to look there.

DID YOU KNOW **that twentysomethings are a lot more intent on saving for retirement than their parents? Among 18- to 34-year-olds, 24 percent started saving for retirement before they turned 20, whereas only 4 percent of people 50 and older started saving that young.** (Jeff Brown, "Twentysomethings Don't Need to Save at Expense of Fun," Knight Ridder/Tribune News Service, February 22, 1999).

10 Things
Worth Breaking Your Piggy Bank For

An amazing date

A concert with your favorite
musician or band

Your IRA

A laptop

A visit to the dentist

A MINI Cooper

A gift for someone who needs it

New clothes

Your iPod

Tunes to go with your iPod

THAT'S SO TAXING

Though we're not all related, every American has one uncle in common. His name is Uncle Sam. Every April 15, Uncle Sam makes his annual visit. He's a tall man with broad shoulders and two very large open hands. He expects you to fill his pockets with the money you owe him—every dime, nickel, and penny. If, like Tony Soprano, you fulfill his wishes, then everything will be just fine, at least until next year, when he comes to visit again. But if you somehow forget about his visit, plan on being out of town, or don't answer the door when he comes knocking, you may find yourself in deep and expensive trouble.

The best way to prepare for Uncle Sam's visit is to have your employer make sure that all of your taxes are being taken out of your paycheck. You can even elect to have a little extra taken out of each paycheck in case you have a sudden windfall of income. If nothing in your income changes, then when you file your taxes [on or before April 15], you'll get a refund, which you can save or use to buy a large Slushee at 7-Eleven. Your choice.

If you're a self-starter and own or operate your own business or work as contract labor, then you need to make sure you're saving enough money to make quarterly payments to Uncle Sam.

Quarterly payments are due:

April 15
June 15
September 15
January 15

The bottom line is to keep Uncle Sam happy. And the best way to keep him happy is to pay your taxes regularly and on time. If all the paperwork is confusing, then hire a tax accountant who can help you calculate your total income and file the appropriate paperwork. The extra hundred or two may seem like a lot now, but it can help you avoid more expensive problems in the future.

The Tipping Point

Malcolm Gladwell wrote the best-selling book *The Tipping Point: How Little Things Can Make a Big Difference.* We recommend that you read it. It's informative, insightful, and worth giving up the latest Grisham or Clancy novel to take time to enjoy.

But the real tipping point isn't about little things making a big difference; it's about actually leaving a tip—and something beyond "Pointed-toe shoes are out of fashion" and "You really should see a dermatologist about that one." We're talking about the moolah. So the next time you find yourself in a restaurant, at a hotel that's way out of your league, or on a ski vacation, here's what you should leave behind:

Cab driver: 15%–20%

Valet parking: $1–$5 [think Kia versus BMW]

Concierge: Not required, but if the service is outstanding, hand out a $5

Bellhop: $1–$5 a bag

Doorman: $1–$2 for hailing a cab

Chambermaid/cleaning woman: $1–$5

Room service: Usually the tips and service fees are tagged on to your bill, but if not, you should tip 15%

Restaurant: 15%–20%

Coat check: $1 per item

Restroom attendant: $.50–$1.00 per visit

Caddie: 50% of the caddie fee

Bag boy: $2–$5

Ski instructor: $5–$10 group lesson; $20–$25 private lesson

Spa treatment: 15%–20%

Hairdresser: 15%

All of the above are recommendations, and many of them offer a range. If you're staying in a two-star motel, driving a beater, and playing a round at the local municipal golf course, then you'll want to lean toward the lower end of the ranges suggested above. But if you just checked into the Ritz-Carlton, driving your BMW and planning to spend the weekend on the golf course at Pebble Beach, then you'll want to lean past the higher end of the tipping scale for great service. The real tipping point is this: Tipping rewards great service and ensures that you'll keep receiving great service for your entire stay.

HEALTH

6 Ways to Exercise That Don't Require a Gym

No. 1. Choose the farthest spot in the parking lot. You'll not only get a brisk walk, but you'll also protect your paint job.

No. 2. Select a basket rather than a cart the next time you go to the grocery store. You'll get a workout for your arms by carrying your groceries around the store. And you'll probably end up buying less food.

No. 3. Keep a pair of hand weights in your living room next to the couch. The next time you're watching reruns of *Seinfeld*, *Friends*, or *Trading Spaces*, do some arm curls and sit-ups. It won't kill you.

No. 4. Land a spot on the TV show *Survivor*. They'll put you on a strict diet and exercise program as you try to survive in the wilderness with some slightly unbalanced and greedy teammates.

No. 5. Quit driving. Yep. You read it here first. Instead, hop on your bike. Or take a walk.

No. 6. Begin stealing purses. You'll have to run in order to avoid the old ladies, kind strangers, and cops. [Beware: Not recommended for people who don't like to serve jail time.]

DID YOU KNOW you can locate a health club in a city you're visiting before you step on a plane? Simply visit www.healthclubs.com. With nearly 6,000 gyms around the world and driving directions included, you don't have an excuse not to work out.

Isn't Pizza a Food Group?

Easy ways to justify fast food:

Pizza—It incorporates all five food groups:

Meat – pepperoni, sausage, Canadian bacon

Dairy – mozzarella, Parmesan

Fruit – tomato sauce [yes, it's a fruit], pineapple

Vegetables – mushrooms, black olives,
green peppers, onions

Grain – thin or thick crust

**Burgers—Also a well-balanced meal:
meat, roll, and salad.**

French fries—It's just potatoes and a little oil. People have been eating and surviving on potatoes for hundreds of years.

Soda—Bottled water and soda cost the same, so how could a little extra flavor do any harm?

Milkshake—It's part of your osteoporosis prevention program.

DID YOU KNOW there's a tie between work and health? A recent Japanese study found that men who worked 60 hours a week were twice as likely to have a heart attack as those who put in 40 hours.

DID YOU KNOW grown-ups are afraid of the dentist, too? Approximately 23 percent of Americans stay away from the dentist because of fear.

FAD DIETS

CAN CABBAGE CAUSE CANCER?

If you're looking for a fad diet, you have an endless list to choose from. Here are just a few:

Grapefruit Diet	Blood Type Diet
Cabbage Soup Diet	Starvation Diet
The Portfolio Diet	Rice Diet
The Scarsdale Diet	Banana Diet
Popcorn Diet	Beverly Hills Diet

10 Signs You're on a Fad Diet

➤ You are filling your grocery cart with only one or two foods that you never really liked in the first place.

➤ The diet promises that you'll look like Courtney Cox, Jennifer Anniston, or any of the other characters on *Friends* [except Joey] within two weeks.

➤ Part of the diet is air.

➤ The diet makes you crave the food you ate in the junior high cafeteria.

➤ Small birds are eating more food than you.

➤ You don't have to exercise, or if you do, you're spending more time in the gym than asleep in bed at night.

➤ The success of the diet depends on you taking small, very expensive pills three to five times a day.

➤ The ads for the diet feature before and after photos—and the photos obviously aren't of the same person.

➤ After the second day of the diet, you're already ready to quit.

➤ The diet fails to mention the true secret of weight loss: Eat less and exercise more.

IT'S ALL IN THE ROGAINE

Fact: About 90 percent of the hair on a person's scalp is growing at any one time.

Fact: Scalp hair grows about one-half inch a month.

Fact: As people age, their rate of hair growth slows.

Fact: Natural blondes typically have more hair [140,000 hairs] than brunettes [105,000 hairs] or redheads [90,000 hairs].

Fact: Most hair shedding is due to the normal hair cycle, and losing 50 to 100 hairs per day is normal.

Fact: It's not a good idea to follow the 100 brush strokes a day, because that much brushing damages hair.

Most hair loss is hereditary. Balding or thinning is the most common cause of hair loss, and it can begin at any age. You can inherit it from either your mother or father's side of the family, and today there are several options to combat hair loss:

Drug treatment. A variety of lotions that can be applied to the scalp are available and can spur hair growth. Daily pills are also available.

Hair transplant. During transplant surgery, hair from the follicle-producing parts of the scalp is moved to the thinning areas. Both men and women have undergone this expensive procedure.

Shave your head. While this is less popular among women—except those embracing the Sinead O'Connor look of the early '90s—many men find that using a razor helps disguise the fact that they're going bald.

Wear a hat.

[Facts taken from http://www.aad.org/pamphlets/hairloss.html]

How to Lose
a Quick 5 Pounds

Take water tablets.

Don't drink water for the rest of the day.

Don't eat for three days.

Don't eat anything that isn't green.

Only eat fiber.

Read a diet book instead of eating.

Just drink grapefruit juice.

Find the main road in town and walk
to the end of it.

Lay on the floor and stare at the ceiling
until the pounds melt away.

Note: None of the above is actually recommended.

DID YOU KNOW there are a lot of graduates who are uninsured? According to the U.S. Census Bureau, nearly one in three young adults between the ages of 18 and 24 has no health insurance—the highest proportion of any age group.

LIFE SURVIVAL SKILLS 101

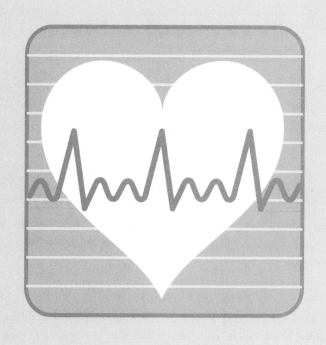

Keeping a Plant Alive
for at Least 12 Months

Keeping a plant alive is much easier said than done. Obviously, it helps to know what kind of plant you're trying to keep alive. If you have the little tag that came with the purchase of your plant, then simply follow the directions. But if you've lost the tag, consider taking it to a local greenhouse to get the plant identified or ask a friend.

Why bother? Because your reputation is on the line. You don't want to be known as someone who can't keep a plant alive, now do you? If you can't keep a plant alive, then how will you care for a pet or spouse down the line?*

If you're a looking at your little green friend and don't have a clue what to do, here are a few hints. Your plant needs the following:

> **Light**
> **Water**
> **Soil**

Though a few plants prefer shady areas, most plants enjoy sunlight. Place your plants in an area where they can enjoy direct sunlight without getting sunburned.

If you water your plant too much or not enough, you'll kill it. So watch how the amount and frequency of water are affecting your plant. If mold is growing on top of the soil, it's too moist. If the leaves are beginning to wilt, it's too dry. You may need to press your finger into the soil to feel the actual moisture level.

Your plant also needs enough soil, which means that if it's outgrowing its current container, it may need an upgrade to a bigger size. You may want to consider fertilizing on a regular basis too. Whatever fertilizer you choose, don't forget to dilute it as per the instructions or else you'll burn the roots of your plant.

Last resort: If you find that, despite your best efforts, your plant is wilting, losing leaves, or dying, then give it to friend who is actually good with plants and can bring it back to life.

*Don't let anyone give you this guilt trip, including us. Some people will never be able to keep a plant alive. That doesn't mean they shouldn't adopt a pet or not get married. It simply means they need to invest in artificial plants and trees. Just stay away from the cheap, plastic, tacky ones.

WINNING AT TRIVIA GAMES

Ken Jennings taught us all a thing or two. The software developer from Salt Lake City, Utah, spent more than six months on *Jeopardy* racking up more right answers and money than anyone in the history of the show.

Two of the most common questions Jennings was asked were, "Do you read the encyclopedia?" and "Did you cram for *Jeopardy*?" Jennings answered "no" on both fronts. He simply described himself as naturally curious, so when he became interested in something he'd take the time to learn more about it. And as far as cramming for *Jeopardy*, it's impossible—the topics and questions are just too broad. Either you know it or not. Rather, Jennings said he learned that the buzzer was actually a bigger factor than he anticipated. Ring in too early and you get locked out of answering the question and ring in too late and someone else will get the right answer.

But eventually—after a winning streak of 74 shows—Jennings finally lost. The final *Jeopardy* question, under the category Business & Industry was:

Most of this firm's 70,000 seasonal white-collar employees work only four months a year.

Jennings answered, "Fed Ex."

The correct answer—provided by contestant Nancy Zerg—was "H&R Block."

Let's face it, you can't be right all the time. But Jennings was right enough to bring home more than $2.5 million dollars on the show. Not bad for a little trivia. So whether you're considering *Jeopardy, Who Wants to Be a Millionaire*, or just an old fashioned game of Trivia Pursuit, here are some tips to winning at trivia games:

1. Be naturally curious. If something you read, see on television, or hear in a conversation piques your interest, take time to learn more about it. You don't even have to pick up a dictionary—simply spend a few minutes online and Google the topic.

2. Look for the answer in the question. A lot of trivia questions contain clues concerning the answer. For example, if you're asked what do the chimneys on the March Hare's house look like in *Alice's Adventure in Wonderland?* You can make an educated guess—even if you can't remember the detail—from the fact that the house is owned by a hare or rabbit. The correct answer: ears.

3. Read the headlines. The majority of trivia questions come from events—both past and present—that everyone would have heard about. Look at who won the Oscars, Grammys, and Nobel Prizes. Note who was elected in foreign countries and who brought home gold in the Olympics.

4. Create word associations. If you're asked whether clocks are turned forward or back one hour in the fall, you can remember that the clock "springs" forward in the spring and "falls" back in the fall.

5. Remember Acronyms. If you're trying to remember the five Great Lakes, just think HOMES: Huron, Ontario, Michigan, Erie, and Superior.

Practice, practice, practice. Play trivia games with friends. Watch *Jeopardy* and other trivia based shows. Play online trivia games. The more you play the more you'll know.

Making Sure
Your Goldfish Doesn't Float

Congratulations! You've managed to keep a plant alive. Now it's time to move on to the next level: keeping a goldfish alive. Anyone can do that—right? Absolutely! But keeping a goldfish alive and giving a goldfish a quality life are two different things.

So here's the insider secret on goldfish:

> Most adult goldfish grow to be six to eight inches long.

That means that the itty-bitty bowl you bought isn't going to keep Goldy happy for very long. One of the reasons goldfish stay small is because those cheap two- or three-gallon bowls stunt the fish's growth. Most goldfish owners know that if they overfeed their fish, then they'll have to clean the bowl more often. See the diagram below:

Thus, most goldfish are involuntarily on a diet and end up surviving for just a year or two rather than the six to nine [and even up to ten] years they're designed to live.

So if you're going to buy a goldfish, spring for the ten-gallon tank and make sure it has a good filter. You'll get to watch Goldy double in size over and over again.

DID YOU KNOW you're not the only one having a bad day? For a quick reminder and laugh, visit www.slipups.com which lists blunders in film, television, books, politics and just about anywhere.

How to Change a Flat Tire

If you ever hear a popping sound or feel your car pulling heavily to one side as you're driving, it's time to pull over. More than likely, you have a flat tire. If you are near a gas station or town with lots of kind people, you can probably flash a smile or a look of desperation and find someone to help you change your tire. But what happens if you're in the middle of nowhere and you get a flat? Everyone needs to know how to change a flat tire.

Before you experience a flat, there are a few things you should do to prepare yourself:

* Locate your spare tire. These extra tires are usually tucked away under the floor of the trunk, or if you're driving a truck, it may be under the rear of the vehicle. Make sure the spare tire has air in it and is in good condition. Also check to see that you have a jack and lug nut wrench, especially if you bought your car used. Ideally, your lug nut remover should be shaped like a cross and include a pry end on one of the spokes to help remove the wheel cover.

* Invest in a can of Fix-A-Flat. This one purchase, which only costs a few dollars, can be used to inflate and preserve your tire until you can get to someone who can change the tire for you!

* Invest in a can of WD-40. This can help loosen lug nuts.

* Pull out your owner's manual and look for specifics on how to change a tire on your particular vehicle.

If the Fix-A-Flat doesn't work and you don't have a cell phone, you'll have to change the tire yourself. Here are some steps to remember:

Make sure your car is parked on a flat surface away from traffic.

Don't forget to use the parking brake and hazard lights. If you have an automatic transmission, place the car in park, but if you have a manual transmission, place it in reverse.

Use the flat end of your lug nut wrench to pry off the hubcap. If you don't have hubcaps [those flat covers on the outside of your wheel well], you can skip this step.

Loosen the lug nuts with your lug nut wrench. Don't take them off all the way.

Look for a stable spot underneath the vehicle to jack it up. Look for a flat metal area underneath the rear of the car. Lift the car no more than one inch off the ground. [Helpful Hint: Owner's manuals will often have diagrams showing you exactly where to jack up the vehicle.]

Remove the flat tire. Replace it with the spare.

Tighten the lug nuts until firm. Do not use excess force.

Lower the car down gently until the vehicle rests completely on the wheels and remove the jack.

Tighten the lug nuts as tightly as possible. Preferably tighten one and then the opposite lug to the one you tightened in a starlike pattern.

Don't worry about placing your hubcap back on. If it's loose, you may lose it.

Replace all tools back in your vehicle.

Drive to the nearest gas station or your home and have your tire replaced. If you have a temporary spare [which is thinner than other tires and sometimes called a "doughnut"], don't drive excessively fast. Do not use a temporary spare or doughnut with a four-wheel drive vehicle, but if you must, do not drive faster than 10 miles per hour.

DID YOU KNOW your dog, cat, or pet rhino may be able to go on vacation after all? Simply visit www. petswelcome.com, a database of over 25,000 pet-friendly hotels, resorts, and beaches. You'll find a list of vaccination requirements if you're traveling abroad as well as any quarantine policies.

DID YOU KNOW there's a special holiday to celebrate your friends? In 1935, the U.S. Congress proclaimed the first Sunday in August as National Friendship Day. It remains a tradition observed in many countries and cultures around the world.

THE HEIMLICH MANEUVER

Scenario No. 1:

You're all alone. You're choking. You can't breathe. You can't call out for help. What do you do? Use the Heimlich maneuver on yourself.

Step 1: Make your hand into a fist and place the thumb side of your fist against your upper stomach, below the ribcage and above the navel.

Step 2: Grab your fist with your other hand and press into your upper stomach. Use a fast, upward thrust. If you can't manage this maneuver, then find something with an edge—like the back of a chair or edge of a table and press your upper stomach against it with a fast, upward thrust. Repeat the thrust until the object is freed from your windpipe.

Step 3: Go to the hospital and see a physician.

Scenario No. 2:

Your friend is choking. Your friend can't breathe. Your friend can't speak. What do you do? Use the Heimlich maneuver.

Step 1: Do not slap the back of the victim as this can make the situation worse. Make your hand into a fist and place the thumb side of your fist against your friend's upper stomach, below the ribcage and above the navel.

Step 2: Wrap your arms around your friend and grab your fist with your other hand and press into the upper stomach. Use a fast, upward thrust. Repeat the thrust until the object is set free. Avoid squeezing the ribcage, which can break your friend's ribs. [Note: Breaking ribs is bad. Real bad.]

Step 3: Go to the hospital and see a physician.

Quick History: In 1974, Dr. Henry Heimlich first described an emergency technique for expelling foreign material blocking the trachea. Now called the Heimlich maneuver, the process is a standard part of first-aid courses.

Don't Let Choking Friends Go to the Bathroom Alone: Every year about 3,000 adults die because they accidentally inhale rather than swallow food. So if you're at dinner, and someone at your table goes to the bathroom because they're embarrassed that they're choking—go with them. You may end up saving a life.

UNFORGETABLE HOLIDAYS

NEVER, EVER FORGET . . .

Mother's Day is the second Sunday in May
Father's Day is the third Sunday in June

MARK YOUR CALENDAR . . .

January is National Soup Month
February is National Pet Dental Health Month
March is National Caffeine Awareness Month
April is National Frog Month
May is National Barbeque Month
June is National Iced Tea Month
July is Anti-Boredom Month
August is National Inventors Month
September is National Little League Month
October is National Toilet Tank Repair Month
November is Good Nutrition Month
December is National Tie Month

HOW COULD YOU FORGET?

February 11—It's Make a New Friend Day
March 26—It's Make up Your Own Holiday Day
April 22—Earth Day
June 6—National Yo-Yo Day
June 13—National Juggling Day
August 6—National Fresh Breath Day
December1—World AIDS Day

HOLLYWOOD BIRTHDAYS . . .

January 25 is Alicia Keys's birthday
February 7 is Ashton Kutcher's birthday
February 17 is Paris Hilton's birthday
March 30 is Norah Jones's birthday
April 30 is Kirsten Dunst's birthday
July 9 is Tom Hanks's birthday
August 16 is Madonna's birthday
September 8 is Pink's birthday
September 27 is Avril Lavigne's birthday
October 4 is Alicia Silverstone's birthday
November 4 is P. Diddy's birthday
November 30 is Clay Aiken's birthday
December 18 is Steven Spielberg's birthday

DID YOU KNOW there are people who actually claim they don't receive any spam? An article in March 2004 Kiplinger's found 7 percent of adults say they receive no spam in their personal email accounts. The rest of us must make up for it. Especially since the average Internet user receives 155 unsolicited email messages every week.

Your Signature Meal

If you don't have one by now, it's time to develop a signature meal. Or at least a signature dish—something great that you can take to parties, dinners, and events on the fly. But that doesn't mean that it has to take all day to make or require really exotic or expensive ingredients. A signature meal only has two requirements: It tastes great and you make it more than once!

Your signature dish is going to fall into one of four categories:

```
Appetizer
Main dish
Side dish
Dessert
```

So ask yourself—what do you like to cook? What makes you feel like a superstar when you serve it? What do people give you the most feedback about?

Maybe it's a particular salad or an Italian dish. Maybe you bake bread or brownies or one decadent chocolate cake. Or maybe you make some mean nachos or grill like a master. That's a sign you've found your signature meal.

But if you're still thinking, *none of these are me*, then here are a few ideas to get you started:

➤ Get a recipe off of the label of a trusted product you buy. These are usually tried and true simple recipes. Plus, if you find one that looks good, you probably already have one of the ingredients required. Some suggestions: Toll House

Morsels, Betty Crocker cake mixes, and Quaker Oats all have some great recipes on them. You can learn how to make a seven-layer dip from some cans of refried beans or chili from a can of diced tomatoes.

➤ Watch the Food Network. The next time you're up way too late, skip the infomercials and watch a chef instead. You'll learn insider's tips on cooking and pick up a few new recipes.

➤ Call Mom or Dad or Grandma or someone else you know who knows how to cook really well. Ask them for some advice and a great recipe.

➤ Pick a recipe and go for it. Test it on a friend or two before taking it to a party. If it doesn't go over well, be willing to try again.

➤ Remember that presentation adds the ooh-ahh factor to any dish. If you're making a dessert, sprinkle some candy or whipped cream on top. If it's an appetizer, spruce up the dish with parsley or cilantro. And try to find a supercool serving dish for whatever you bring.

➤ If all else fails, then stop by the deli counter at your local supermarket.

DID YOU KNOW the largest seller of clothing isn't Gucci, Prada, or Chanel? According to the Wall Street Journal, it's Wal-mart—whose sales account for around 25 percent of the U.S. apparel market.

Wrapping Gifts

So They Look Like They're Worth Something

You may not be able to spring for the new $100-gift your friend really wanted, but that doesn't mean you can't make your gift look like a hundred bucks—at least on the outside. To spruce up your wrapping techniques, try a few of the following:

❋ Buy a piece of fabric or cloth and a simple silk ribbon. Secure the gift inside the cloth with a bow.

❋ Purchase a gift bag. It's the faithful standby for last-minute gift-wrapping. Buy a nice bag and a package of tissue paper. Layer the inside of the bag with the tissue paper, add your gift, and don't forget to sign the card.

❋ Go for the box. Monte Hall on *Let's Make a Deal* asked contestants if they wanted Door No. 1, Door No. 2, Door No. 3, or the box. When it comes to gift-wrapping, always go for the box when it's available. To determine the amount of wrapping paper you need, place the gift in the middle of the sheet of wrapping paper and fold the paper over until you have enough to cover the entire box. Cut along the folded lines. Fold the paper lengthwise along your gift and tape the edges together with clear tape. On each end of the gift, pinch the sides together to make a triangle-like shape and tape to the sides of the box. Once you're done, add a ready-made bow and gift card.

✳ Attach an extra gift. You can add to the gift you're giving by attaching a small extra gift, such as a piece of candy, an ornament, or a small piece of jewelry to the outside of the wrapping.

 Gift-wrapping Don'ts:

- No comic strips
- Absolutely no toilet paper
- No tin foil

- No wax paper
- No brown paper bags
- No paper towels

MOVE OVER AMERICAN IDOL:

HOW TO BE ROCKSTAR

So Simon says your voice is the worst thing he's heard since, well, the last contestant he told that to three minutes ago. You pick yourself off the carpet of rejection and decide you're going to make your rock-star dreams come true. Here's a few tips for your journey to fame:

1. *Keep practicing.* Study music—all different types. Listen to it 24/7. And keep strumming your guitar, beating your drums, or humming on your harmonica every chance you get. If you get an opportunity to play somewhere, take it, even if it's at the senior center with an audience of four deaf people.

2. *Keep your day job.* It takes a while to make it in the music business, so make sure you have other streams of income. Use your paychecks to help buy the equipment you need for your band. But in the end, remember that the music business is just that, a business. And in order for you to make money, your skills and talents are going to have to make someone else money.

3. *Try not to sound like everyone else.* Sure, you can have your groove, whether it's pop, urban, hip-hop, alternative, grunge, classic, whatever, but you need to add an edge to it that makes it your own. Remember that only you're the only one on the planet that can make the music that's reflective of you. Don't despise your uniqueness.

4. ***Keep it humble.*** Just because you experience some mild success doesn't mean it's time to start thrashing hotel rooms. Keep being the nice guy or gal. It will take you further than you will ever imagine.

5. ***Make a demo.*** If you're going to find an executive ear in L.A., Nashville, or anywhere, then you're going to need a sample of your work. Save up. Make a recording. Be ready to give it to anyone who is willing to listen.

6. ***Keep the dream alive.*** There's nothing wrong with wanting to be a rock star, but remember that life changes and priorities change. You may one day discover you'd rather stick to playing the local circuit close to home or use your talents to encourage others. Remember that the dream of being a rock star is more about the rock than the stardom. So whatever you do and wherever you go, keep making music.

Carry snacks. Think of all the things Scooby-Doo was willing to do for a Scooby snack. Buy a box of pet treats and carry them in your car. Or the next time you're going through the drive-through at your local bank, ask for a few dog biscuits. They may look at you a little funny, but hey, it's worth it.

Be persistent. Some dogs, and especially cats, take awhile to warm up to new people. Don't take it personally. Just remember that by continually being kind, gentle, and patient with that funny little animal, you're bound to win its heart.

Get down on their level. If you're sitting or lying on the floor, pets are more likely to come up and check you out.

Act comfortable. It's important not to let any fear show when you're being introduced to an animal. Act like it's no big deal, even if it is!

Kibbles 'n Bits of Wisdom

When you reach toward a dog, avoid reaching over its head. This is a sign of dominance and not well received during a time of anxiety. It's a good way to get bit. Instead, reach under the chin.

Using a high, squeaky voice with animals can help.

Cats are too smart or too stubborn to be bribed with treats. If you run into a scaredy-cat, then try scratching under its chin and at the base of its tail if you can get close enough.

Some younger cats can be engaged by playful activity. Use a string or piece of cloth and give them something to chase.

THRIFT STORE GALORE

Whether you're a treasure hunter or a recent graduate in need of some cheap stuff, thrift stores can offer you an incredible selection of merchandise at prices you just can't beat. The best part about thrift stores is that the merchandise is constantly changing, and you can stumble upon collectibles, vintage clothing, furniture, and household items at dirt-cheap prices. Some thrift stores offer special savings days—with 25 percent or 50 percent off everything bought on a particular day. Other stores place colored stickers on their older items and color-code the discounts. Most are just looking to turn over their merchandise, so if you're willing to hunt, you can find some underpriced goods that you can resell on eBay and make a quick buck.

You CAN $AVE

Avoiding
Plumber's Crack
FASHION TIPS FOR THE
BIG LOTS SHOPPER

Never shop alone. It's dangerous out there.

*Always shop with a trusted friend who
will tell you the truth.*

*Just because you think it will fit when you lose ten
pounds doesn't mean that it ever will.*

*Fluorescent is out and it's not ever
coming back in [hopefully!].*

*Just because it's a bargain doesn't
mean it's a good deal.*

*If you really need to buy those baggy pants,
buy a belt at the same time.*

Winning the White Elephant

DEFINITION: **white elephant** *n.* 1a. A rare, expensive possession that is a financial burden to maintain. 1b. Something of dubious or limited value. 2. An article, ornament, or household utensil no longer wanted by its owner. 3. An endeavor or venture that proves to be a conspicuous failure. 4. A rare whitish or light-gray form of the Asian elephant, often regarded with special veneration in regions of Southeast Asia and India.

—*The American Heritage® Dictionary of the English Language, Fourth Edition*

Every year around the holidays, the white elephant makes an appearance.

If you're unfamiliar with a white elephant gift exchange, let us clue you in.

Every participant in the gift exchange brings a specially wrapped gift to the event. Nothing is labeled, so no one knows who brought which gift. The game begins with contenders drawing numbers written on slips of paper. The person who draws #1 selects a gift and opens it so everyone can see what it is. Then the person with #2 gets to take the unwrapped gift from #1 or choose a gift that hasn't been selected yet. Person #3 and those following get to choose any unwrapped gift or choose a gift that is still wrapped. After the last person with the highest number finally chooses, the first person can steal a gift according to the rules [since this is their first opportunity], and the game continues until someone accepts the gift given up by the first person.

Two rules maintain some order in the midst of this chaos:

✳ A gift can be stolen only once in any given turn.

✳ The third owner of a gift gets to keep it and it can't be stolen again.

There are really only three ways to win at a white elephant exchange:

1. Draw #1 and get the final choice on whose gift you'd like to keep.
2. When you get a really cool gift, pretend like it's a dud so that no one else wants it.
3. Forget about the gift you're getting and focus on the gift you're giving. Either bring something really cool and desirable or something terrible and disastrous to the event and see who fights over the item or, better yet, gets stuck with it.

white elephant: An unwanted or useless item, as in *The cottage at the lake had become a real white elephant—too run down to sell, yet costly to keep up,* or *Grandma's ornate silver is a white elephant; no one wants it— but it's too valuable to discard.* This expression comes from a legendary former Siamese custom whereby an albino elephant, considered sacred, could only be owned by the king. The king would bestow such an animal on a subject with whom he was displeased and wait until the high cost of feeding the animal, which could not be slaughtered, ruined the owner. The story was told in England in the 1600s, and in the 1800s the term began to be used figuratively.

—*The American Heritage Dictionary*

WRAP IT UP

With more than $5 billion worth of gift wrap tossed in the garbage every year, the idea of recycling things you already have to wrap gifts may seem like a good idea. But before you go overboard, here are a few things you probably shouldn't wrap your next gift with (unless, of course, it's a white elephant exchange).

Tin Foil

Toilet Paper

The bag that came with the purchase

A Used T-Shirt

Paper Towels

Fast Food Hamburger Wrapper

Plastic Wrap

Wall Paper

Wet Newspaper

Old Bed Linens

The Box of a More Expensive Product

A Used Dish Towel

Deerskin

THE ULTIMATE
IN THANK-YOU NOTES

Here's a little secret: Thank-you notes improve the quantity and the quality of the gifts you receive. People like to be acknowledged for the kind things they do—and while an e-mail and a phone call are both great expressions, a thank-you note provides a tangible form for expressing gratitude. So whether someone gives you a $5-check for your birthday or a $500-gift certificate for your graduation, the person deserves a handwritten—yes, you have to skip the word processor—thank-you note.

If you don't have stationery, then you need to invest in a small package of cards. You'll want small ones because it's really hard to fill up a big card with lots of gushy words. When you make your card selection, you may be leaning toward the Winnie the Pooh or race car driver-themed cards, but you need to find something that can be used to express yourself in personal and in business situations [or buy appropriate cards for each—you big spender, you].

When you're writing the actual message, begin by acknowledging the person's name. It can be as simple as "Aunt Thelma" or "Dear Bob," but you need to let the person know the message is personalized at the beginning of the note. Your first sentence should acknowledge the gift you received. You may want to say something such as, "Thank you for the green ukulele slipcover." Then mention how the gift will be used. "It will make carrying the ukulele to events much easier, because of the protective layering." Now you don't need to lie. Even if you think the new ukulele slipcover is the color of vomit and you already have two, you can still point out the positive features of the gift. Then acknowledge the reason and relationship behind the gift. You may want to say, "It was so great having you at my graduation ceremony. I am glad you were there." Then close with a simple "Thank you again for the gift." And add a "Respectfully," "Sincerely," or "Love," and sign your name.

So your message will look something like this:

Dear Bob,

    Thank you for the green ukulele slipcover. It will make carrying the ukulele to events much easier because of the protective layering. It was so great to have you at my graduation ceremony. I am glad you were there.

Love,
Milfred

    Most important, send your thank-you notes quickly! Don't wait. They'll be doubly appreciated.

Keeping New Year's
Resolutions Next Year

How many New Year's resolutions have you made over the years? How many have you actually been able to keep past February? Whether you're trying to lose weight, get a new job, or change your habits, you're going to need to do something a little different this year if you're going to make a permanent change.

1st, you need to have a plan of action. You can resolve to lose fifteen pounds, but if you don't develop a plan of how to change your eating and/or exercise patterns, the poundage isn't going to budge. Commit to taking a walk after dinner. Switch to diet soda. Join the gym and actually go on regular basis. Get a partner and begin lifting weights. Avoid buying desserts at the grocery store. Develop a plan that includes specific action as part of your resolution.

2nd, post reminders of the resolution around your home and workplace. It may only be January 28, but it's easy to forget what you were so pumped up about changing in your life just a month before. You need to remind yourself of your goal and why you've established it. You may want to get out of debt so you can start putting money away for a car or a home. You may want to buy a wedding ring or just be able to pay for a date with that cute neighbor who lives three doors down. Make yourself a few three-by-five cards that remind you of your goal and put them in places where you'll see them around the house. Jot the goal on a few Post-it notes and place one on the refrigerator and another on the bathroom mirror. You'll find these reminders more than helpful.

3rd, let some friends in on your little resolution. Better yet, find a friend with the same resolution and hold each other accountable. Making a change in your lifestyle takes time, and a little help from a friend can make all the difference.

If all else fails and you just can't keep the resolution, don't be discouraged. There's always next year.

CREATIVE THEME PARTIES

Tired of the same old boring weekends? Movie-and-pizza blues got you down? Try these party ideas to add some spice to your next gathering:

Olé!—Decorate with bright colors and serve nachos, tacos, and other Tex-Mex favorites. Spring for a piñata and watch your friends turn into kids again as they try to hit the swinging donkey. Have a jalapeno-eating contest [similar to "Chubby Bunny"].

Decade Fun—Return to the '70s for a groovy evening of disco, Twister, and world peace. Assign teams or individuals wacky topics such as ingredients for the perfect 'fro or John Travolta dance moves from *Grease* and watch the creativity flow. Vary the theme by throwing an '80s bash with big hair, leg warmers, parachute pants, and Michael Jackson music, or a '90s rave with grunge gear, baggy pants, and Rollerblades.

New Job or Raise Praise—When a friend or tribe member has cause to celebrate, plan an elegant dinner in their honor. Wear business suits and set the table with all the utensils of a five-star restaurant. [You can look up instructions for place settings online . . . I mean, honestly, *who* really knows all that stuff?] Serve a lovely green salad, and then when it's time for the main course, bring out grandly presented hot dogs with ketchup drizzled across the plate in swirls. Tell your guest of honor that no matter how Mr. or Mrs. Big Britches they get, they will always be just a bunch of unmentionable parts rolled together to make one big hot dog!

Behind the Entertainment—Invite people to bring one or two of their favorite songs, scenes from movies, magazine articles, or book chapters. Take turns sharing each one and why you like it so much. This fun party idea can range from funny to serious, silly to spiritual. Just let it flow and see what happens. Variations could include giving them a theme ahead of time and asking them to bring media that match it [try *love, airplanes, pirates, dogs,* or *sacrifice,* for example] or using the props people bring to play your own version of *Whose Line Is It Anyway?*

You can have fun, make memories, laugh, and celebrate without breaking the bank. You just have to get a little creative sometimes.

CHEAP AIRLINE TICKETS

If you're looking for cheap airline tickets, it's time to go online.
Here are a few sites you won't want to miss:

www.skyauction.com
www.lowestfare.com
www.travel.yahoo.com
www.statravel.com
www.cheapseatstravel.com
www.hotwire.com
www.orbitz.com
www.travelocity.com
www.expedia.com
www.qixo.com
www.sidestep.com
www.cheaptickets.com
www.priceline.com
www.mobissimo.com

Other tips:

➤ Book your trip at least 21 days in advance.

➤ If you're flexible, consider bidding on a site such as www.price-line.com or www.hotwire.com.

➤ Leave and return on a midweek day.

➤ Watch for sales even after you buy. If your ticket price drops, some airlines will refund the difference.

➤ Consider staying an extra day or leaving a day earlier to reduce the cost of the ticket.

➤ Switch airports. Search for airports within an hour's drive—you may save hundreds of dollars.

➤ Always collect frequent-flyer miles. They add up!

COMMON PROBLEMS
& UNCOMMON SOLUTIONS

Problem: A rainbow of mold growing on base of the shower curtain.
Solution: Buy a new shower curtain. Or better yet, take the old curtain and throw it in the washing machine on gentle cycle with a cap full of detergent. It should come out clean and mold-free. NOTE: Do not let your roommate or yourself place the shower curtain in the dryer. Bad things will happen. Guaranteed.

Problem: Mailbox is always empty except for bills.
Solution: Reach out and touch someone. Not inappropriately, of course. But pick up a pen, write a letter, jot an email, dial the phone. The best way to get cards and letters is to send them. You can also make new friends by going on line and Googling key words such as "pen pal" and "letter exchange." You may also want to form a pen pal relationship with troops overseas. If you send out a few letters, it won't be long until your mailbox is full.

Problem: Knowing how to comfort a friend who has lost a loved one.
Solution: Reach out through a phone call, card, and visit to let them know you care. Remember that being a good listener is sometimes the most powerful thing you can do. Give the person the time they need to grieve. Don't try to rush them through the process. And always ask if there's anything you can do to help.

Problem: Not enough space to entertain.
Solution: Buy a fold-up table and chairs. Throw an inexpensive table cloth on it from Target and voilá . . . you're back in business.

Problem: You still don't know how to dance.

Solution: Check out any local restaurants or places that may offer free introductory dance classes. Look up dance studios in your local phone book. Call around to see what types of classes and styles of dance are available. Observe a class if you're not sure which to choose. Invite a friend or two to join in. And remember that it's all about having fun.

Problem: You realize its time to downsize, but the task seems daunting.

Solution: Take it one day at a time. Make a goal to unload a box a day. Donate it to good will. Drop it off at a "trading assistant" who will unload the goods on eBay in exchange for a percentage of the profits. Think twice before you make future purchases. After all, do you really, really need it?

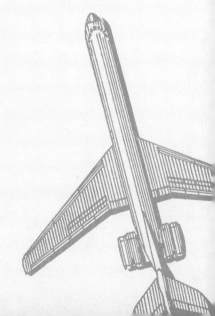

About the Authors

Margaret Feinberg is an outdoor enthusiast and avid traveler who is still learning what it means to conquer her world. She lives in Alaska and writes way too many books during the cold and wet winters. She's written *Twentysomething: Surviving and Thriving in the Real World* (a must-have for anyone in or near their twenties), *Simple Acts of Friendship*, *Simple Acts of Faith*, and *Simple Prayers of Hope* (all of which feature cool Norman Rockwell artwork) as well as some titles for Relevant Books including *God Whispers*. There's a whole lot of other books and articles you can read about at www.margaretfeinberg.com. Now that she's finished this book, she hopes she can keep her next goldfish alive for longer than three months.

Leif Oines is the six-foot-eight Norwegian giant who swept Margaret Feinberg off her feet while she was visiting his hometown in Sitka, Alaska. [Surprise! The authors are married.] He has served as a youth minister, camp counselor, worship leader, and jack-of-all-trades at various churches and summer camps, though he has to work outside the church to support his ministry habit for now. Though this is the first book with his name on the cover, he is taking at least partial credit for the newlywed book, *Just Married,* which Margaret recently completed.

You can reach Margaret and Leif at
margaret@margaretfeinberg.com or by writing

Margaret Feinberg and Leif Oines
P.O. Box 2981
Sitka, AK 99835

P.S. We're huge fans of Compassion International, an organization dedicated to helping children in Third World countries. They have a new initiative to combat the AIDS crisis in Africa that we're particularly excited about. To find out more about Compassion International or to sponsor a child, visit www.compassion.com.

SURVIVING AND
THRIVING IN
THE REAL WORLD

twentysomething

MARGARET FEINBERG
FOREWORD BY BEBO NORMAN

**From life as a student to life in the "real world,"
twentysomething is the only guidebook you need!**

Offering Scriptural insights, encouragement, humor, and practical wis-
dom, *twentysomething* confronts this "crisis" and shows you how to
survive without losing your patience or your
passion for life. *twentysomething* will
inspire you to hold onto your dreams and
to embark fearlessly on the journey God
has for you.